POCKET BOOKS
A Division of Simon & Schuster
1230 Avenue of the Americas
New York, NY 10020

Library of Congress Cataloging-in-Publication Data TK

ISBN: 0-7434-6515-6

First Pocket Books trade paperback printing May 2002

10 9 8 7 6 5 4 3 2 1

POCKET and colophon are trademarks of Simon & Schuster Inc.

Cover art by

Printed in the U.S.A.

For information regarding special discounts for bulk purchases, please contact Simon &
Schuster Special Sales at 1-800-456-6798 or business@simonandschuster.com

Dedication

For Rebecca, my love, my wife, who teaches me to do the right thing

And, for my children, Rachel, Sarah, and Nathan, who I hope will grow up to be good people in a more moral world.

TABLE OF CONTENTS

Introduction

I WROTE THIS BOOK BECAUSE I WANT TO FEEL SAFER in this "every man for himself" world. I need your generosity of spirit to encourage my own. I wrote this book because I believe that you and I can make a difference. I know that you and I can be better. I wrote this book so that your children and mine can be inspired by our goodness.

This is not a book about abstract or philosophical concepts of justice. This is not a book about the loftier conflicts between freedom of speech and the incitement to prejudice it might produce, or affirmative action and the reverse discrimination that it might engender. This is not a book urging that you relinquish the mundane and devote your life to saving rain forests or the hungry children of Rwanda. This is a book about approaching your ordinary relationships and your everyday quandaries with greater empathy, greater sensitivity, greater fairness, and greater kindness.

I am convinced, both as someone who has immersed himself in the subject of genocide, and as a mental health professional who has dealt with individuals attempting to find a satisfying life path, that everyday moral behavior must be addressed. It is commonplace decency that will lay the foundation for a better society.

Let's begin with a self-evaluation.

How many of the following thoughts have crossed your mind?

I know that what I'm doing is wrong, but I can't help myself.

I wish I could be a better person.

I know what I should do, but I don't do it.

I'm torn between my loyalty to him and my concern for her.

When it comes right down to it, it's every man for himself.

I can't relate to your problem because I've never experienced it.

I'm better than she is.

I've got my own problems. I don't want to hear about yours.

I want to do the right thing, but sometimes I don't know what the right thing is.

Everybody bends the rules. I'd be a jerk not to.

What you're doing is wrong. But who am I to judge?

What you're about to do is self-destructive. But it's your life.

Why should I do that for you? The last time I asked you for help, you didn't come through for me.

What you did is unforgivable. I'll never be your friend again.

I know I hurt you, but I just don't want to apologize.

I don't want to ask for help.

I want to express my feelings whenever I have them.

I wish I were married to her (his) spouse.

If some, or many, of the above sound familiar, your moral self cries out for your attention.

You have been told that the secret to feeling good is to be kinder and more generous to yourself. Perhaps you have even come to believe that if you only had X or Y or Z, you could find inner peace and personal fulfillment. Tragically, you may dismiss self-respect because you have not yet attained a certain measure of success. (And, anyway, to liberally paraphrase Walker Percy in *The Second Coming:* We can become a professor, discover the secret of the universe, win a Pulitzer prize, make ten million dollars, emerge victorious in an international decathlon, or write the novel of the century, and still flunk life.)

I offer you a different way, a different remedy—a remedy that does not demand any achievement or acquisition to feel good about yourself. It only requires that you do what is right, what is fair. It only asks that you be generous. It only wants you to be your best.

Many of us have the sense that so much of our potential is unrealized. But we have overlooked a basic need in our quest for self-realization. I would suggest that a vital reason for our lack of personal fulfillment is that we have not given sufficient heed to our moral selves.

I believe you want to do what is right. And, in many instances, your instincts have probably led you to moral decisions. You view yourself as a fundamentally good person. But the key word here is *fundamentally*. That is, you acknowledge that there are times when you falter, when you behave in ways that even *you* know are questionable.

Unfortunately, there are many occasions when you also deceive yourself. In order to maintain a positive self-perception, you rationalize acting in ways that are dishonest, unkind, or selfish. It is easiest for you to forgive your immoral behavior when you have been hurt by another. But you also find startlingly convenient rationales for your unfair behavior toward those who have never done you any harm as well.

You tell yourself those are "gray areas," that a case can be made for acting as you did "under the circumstances." You provide yourself with excuses in order to squelch any potential pangs of guilt.

Everybody does that *sometimes*.
People do worse things than this.
Nobody's perfect.
It will be better in the long run.
It's not such a big deal.
He's such a jerk. He deserved it anyway.

I don't know what came over me.
I wasn't going to, but then . . .
I *had* to.

We engage in all sorts of psychological somersaults in order to remain blameless, in order to retain our self-image of goodness. Ironically,
the fact that we use these excuses to justify our behavior implies that,
deep down, we know what is right and wrong, just and unjust.

When we see another acting in the same unjust manner, we quickly
condemn him. We have little difficulty making black and white judgments of our fellow man or woman. We don't look for extenuating
circumstances that might have caused her to behave as she did. Did
her husband scold her unfairly when she left for work in the morning?
Was she sleep-deprived because her child was throwing up throughout
the night? Was she on edge because she had just been informed that
she will probably lose her job? No, we don't ponder the possibilities.
We excuse our own actions when our intentions are honorable or, at
least, benign. We judge others simply by what they do. And how easily
we succumb to feeling morally superior to them.

But fairness requires that we all become more reticent to judge.
It is remarkable how easily we form impressions based on superficial
information, and how resistant those impressions are to change. After
you have so quickly decided what kind of person I am, you will
tend to disregard or distort input to the contrary, while continuing
to view my behavior through a preconceived lens.

We must become smarter. Traditionally, intelligence has been
viewed as an intellectual construct. That is, the intelligent individual
was someone who possessed a certain body of knowledge, particular
intellectual skills, and a proficiency in comprehending and articulat-
ing abstract concepts. In recent years, we have seen the identification
of a second realm of intelligence — emotional intelligence. Considerable data have implied that particular emotional abilities may be as
vital to personal achievement as intellectual ones.

There is a third realm of intelligence, however, that has even more profound consequences for personal well-being. Moreover, in addition to the effects on individual progress, the consequences of the workings of this domain directly affect the health of our wider society. I am speaking about *moral intelligence.*

Moral intelligence encompasses both the ability to *behave* morally and the capacity to *reason* in a moral manner. All of us have our own ideas about how we would define a highly developed moral individual. But cross-cultural research has indicated that there appear to be certain criteria that are *universally* held: *fairness, duty or a responsibility to others, dignity, and self-control.* These criteria are not tied to any particular religious orientation, nor, as evidenced by their widespread nature, are they culture-bound. Furthermore, as we shall see, the objective of our moral inclination seems to be a dual one. That is, acting morally often serves our own need to self-actualize, as well as registering our concern for others.

Millennia ago, moral prescriptions were not seen as deriving from external authorities such as religion or social coercion. On the contrary, they sprang from our natural desires. In *Rethinking Goodness*, Michael Wallach and Lisa Wallach, both professors of psychology at Duke University, point out:

> Plato and Aristotle held that to be just, self-controlled, and temperate was what we ourselves wanted and was essential to our own well-being and happiness. So did Confucius, in China, and Buddha, in India. For all these thinkers, we were not to be moral because of what gods or other human beings demanded or imposed. Rather, morality represented something of which we ourselves are the authors, but that we often forget or neglect or are confused about. We need to cultivate our moral tendencies, they asserted, but not in order to satisfy some external authority. We should do so because of what we ourselves most want.

Times have changed. Michael Wallach and Lisa Wallach go on to note:

> The death of any but a minimal ethic after liberalism's arrival on the scene was inevitable because of the way morality had come to be—and still mostly is—understood. It tends to be viewed as distinct from human desire or motivation and therefore necessarily impositional. It is a "should," something we are "supposed to do," not something we want to do.

For decades we have lived with a moral relativism that has handcuffed us to undemanding refrains: Don't infringe on another's rights, all opinions are equally valid, all values have merit. Personal morality has been legitimized by personal preferences. Moral debate has been strangled by statements like, "Well, that's just the way I feel!" Feelings have held sway over principles, or reason, for that matter. Morality remained a private affair.

The term *moral intelligence* implies that we must use our moral self in an intelligent manner. That moral self must not be buffeted by transitory impulses, nor controlled by dicta that have been forcibly fed. Moral behavior requires analysis, understanding, and emotional empathy. Doing what's right may preclude an unconsidered expression of emotion or a petty act of revenge that feels satisfying at the moment. Perhaps, most importantly, the moral individual pictures an ideal that is longingly pursued.

In evaluating *fairness*, the question posed is: What is a fair allotment for me *and* the other? The rules of fairness are not rigid ones. They expand as other factors are injected into the situation or as the context evolves. But the idea of fairness must be followed through. Commitments made must be kept. The assumption is made that it is in the long-term interest of both the individual and the stability of society for contracts to be held sacred.

For the morally intelligent person, *the responsibility felt toward*

others is experienced as a personal *duty* and a freely taken obligation. Such a person recognizes that his vista of concern must encompass others as well as himself. Decency requires that he go out of his way.

But decency is dying. A while ago, I approached a neighbor to ask her if she would take the mail out of my box for the next week while I was on vacation. Over the previous three years that we lived in proximity to one another, we had many contacts because our children were playmates. Her reply astonished me: "I guess I could. But when we go away on vacation, we usually pay a teenager down the block to do that for us." Don't bother me and I won't bother you. Don't ask me for any assistance and I won't expect any of you.

A "go it alone approach" has quashed a true concern for anyone else but me or my immediate family. An assumption of the primacy of individual freedom over communal obligations extinguishes any guilt we might otherwise experience for this lapse in decency. Furthermore, we seem to have to work harder and run faster merely to remain in economic place. Our focus, thereby, becomes even more self-centered. How can I expend energy on you when I'm needing increasing amounts simply to survive?

Generosity has been replaced by an unseemly sensitivity to reciprocity. You wonder what you will receive in return for the assistance you rendered. You also fret about your ability to respond to my kindness, as you feel compelled to "balance the books." You are more likely to ask a favor of me if you anticipate being able to reciprocate at some point in the future.

You don't want to owe. It makes you feel less than me. For most of us, the concept of *giving freely* has been supplanted by the apprehension of *burdensome* indebtedness and obligation.

Even in friendship, you measure. You've had Sam and Susan over for dinner three times already, and they've only had you over once, you complain. Who is in debt to whom? you calculate. How quick you are to resent having extended yourself. Several years ago, I was in a carpool with two other families. One of my children became seriously ill, and I asked one of the parents if she could take over my responsibilities for the coming week. "Sure," she replied. And then she added, "Sure, I'll do it for you this week, and you can cover for me the first week in June." *Giving freely.* We look at those who do as suckers.

You so easily voice your compassion. "My heart goes out to him," you sympathetically intone. But, what do you *do* to alleviate his suffering? "If there's anything you need, let me know," you offer. But when you don't hear from him, you simply move on with your life. Is it so difficult to *imagine* what he might need and simply do it without waiting for a formal invitation?

A wise man taught that an *acquaintance* is someone who may be prepared to do something you ask, but only when asked, and only what is specifically asked. A friend, on the other hand, knows you and understands your needs, often before you are aware of them. In many instances, it isn't necessary to ask a friend to do something for you; he or she will have already acted, even before you have asked.

In her book *Rights Talk*, the legal scholar Mary Ann Glendon has pointed to further evidence of insularity in our tendency to define our relation to society primarily in terms of rights, and to define justice as the defense of our rights. Rights, she points out, have supplanted duty. Self has superseded community.

Privacy is certainly a right. But "respecting another's privacy" provides us with another convenient excuse to shirk moral responsibility. An acquaintance, Anne, tells me that a year ago her friend Robert finally landed a job that put him on the "fast track." He threw himself into his work, often spending seventy and eighty hours a week at the office proving his drive and dedication to his superiors. The money started to pour in, which only fed Robert's determination to "make it big." Robert had become a driven man, fueled by fantasies of summer homes, European vacations, limousines, and the envy of his colleagues. The underside, however, was predictable. Robert's wife and children seldom saw him. When they did, he was too tired or preoccupied for any meaningful interaction. Robert missed every single game of his son's high school basketball season and broke his ten-year-old daughter's heart when he failed to show up for her ballet recital. It was clear to Anne that Robert had forsaken his loved ones. And yet, she said nothing to Robert about his values having become skewed, about the abject neglect of his family. "It was not really my place to interfere," she insisted.

At one time or another, you have probably echoed Anne's conclusion, "It's not really my place to interfere." Why did you adopt this hands-off approach? Most likely because you were too frightened of reprisal (If I tell him how to run his life, he might turn around and tell me how to run mine), or too unsure of your moral duty to confront your friend about his selfish actions. Perhaps you simply didn't want to expend the energy. But your friend needed your help, not your indifference.

The third universally held moral precept is *dignity*. When most of us think of dignity, we think about our own dignity. How can I remain in this relationship and keep my sense of dignity? I fret. How can I leave this meeting with my dignity intact? I wonder. The morally intelligent individual is concerned not only with personal dignity, but with encouraging the dignity of those who cross his path. He poses two questions after an interpersonal encounter: (1) Did the other person depart having maintained (or even enhanced) his dignity? and (2) Did I leave the encounter feeling good about how I behaved?

How easily we feel wounded by the slight of another. And how easily we fail to discern our similar unkindness. The question to which we must always return is, "Would I want to be treated that way?" At times, you might deny concern and say, "I don't really care that much if he treats me considerately, as long as he does what I need him to do." But when you offer this absolution, I don't believe you, for you still beg the question, "How would you *want* to be treated?" I am convinced the answer would always be, "With consideration."

Across cultures, it has been observed that the morally intelligent person utilizes *self-control*. He does so because he is aware of lurking impulses that will lead him astray. At indecisive moments in our life, we have oftentimes been exhorted to "Follow your instincts" or "Go with what feels right." The advice has been seductive because it requires little of us and because it allows us to satisfy our momentary needs. But the path that our emotions propel us onto has frequently proven self-defeating. It has taken us to decisions that, in calmer moments, we would have rejected as intemperate. When our behavior is driven solely by feelings, consequences are not fully contemplated. Furthermore, when we are only driven by primal emotions, others' sensibilities are not taken into consideration.

There is no question that it feels good to do what is right. We feel ennobled when we do so. Moreover, it is our own sense of intrinsic worth that forms the basis of our moral *demand* for just treatment by another. Why is it so difficult to see the worth of our neighbor? Why are we seduced by selfish, unkind, and ungenerous impulses?

No one doubts that we all have the potential for goodness as well as evil. But most of us are frightened. Some of us live with omnipresent fears that shadow our everyday movements. Others have buried their primal fears, which, nonetheless, sometimes subtly, sometimes sharply, push them in a certain direction.

What do we fear? We fear not getting enough. We fear not being enough. We fear not doing enough to keep us safe and secure. Of course, what one individual requires in order to feel safe and secure may be vastly different from the requirements of another. But it is our fears that are at the heart of our indiscretions.

When we feel an overriding need to protect ourself, we invariably wind up being insensitive to the feelings of others. When I am anxious, I will push you aside. When I am angry, I will lash out, often hurting innocent bystanders. The greater the anxiety or resentment, the more selfish our orientation will be. *Any* intense emotion can cause us to lose sight of another person's needs and sensibilities. People who are at peace with themselves do not act cruelly toward others.

Before we can act unselfishly, we must be able to empathize.

Mental health professionals agree that empathy is the most significant healing factor in a therapeutic relationship. Empathy is also the most potent generator of a sense of connectedness to another. Empathy entails both the ability to vicariously experience another's emotions and a sympathetic concern for the well-being of another based on an understanding of his perspective. In order to be a good person, you must empower your empathic potential. Chapter One includes an explanation of how our empathy emerges, and offers suggestions for enhancing it.

People have routinely conceived of morality as something opposed to innate tendencies. But there is much evidence to suggest that moral behavior has now become hard-wired. An evolutionary process has culminated in moral propensities becoming a part of our *genetic* makeup. Moral behavior, in other words, does not necessarily rely on fear of punishment or an expectation of reward (either in this world or the world to come). As James Q. Wilson has noted, we are born with a "moral sense."

Observations of very young children clearly indicate that acting morally is not something that requires the suppression of natural desires. Researchers have amassed large numbers of examples of friendliness, of spontaneous sharing, and of sympathy and compassion. Experiencing distress when another is distressed seems primitive, naive, and universal. Psychologists have reported indications of a sensitivity to the distress of others during infancy. Two- and three-day-olds cry when other infants cry, even when they do not cry in response to other, equally loud noises. In addition to crying, ten- to fourteen-month-olds may whimper or silently attend to expressions of distress from another person. Often they respond by soothing themselves or by seeking a parent for comfort. An eleven-month-old girl, upon seeing another child fall and cry, puts her thumb in her mouth and buries her head in her mother's lap.

Between one and two years of age, new behaviors emerge. The toddler may touch or pat another in distress as if to provide solace.

She may seek assistance for the person in distress, or even give her something to provide comfort, such as a cookie, blanket, or teddy bear. Children demonstrate sensitivity to the emotional states and needs of others well before they achieve a sophisticated level of cognitive functioning. We have all probably witnessed the very young child spontaneously walk over and comfort a grieving parent.

Preschool children display more varied and complex responses to the needs of others. In a classic study of sympathy, developmental psychologist Lois Murphy observed that nursery children show a host of reactions to a peer's distress, including comforting and helping the victim, asking questions of the troubled child, punishing the agent of the child's distress, protecting the victim, and asking an adult for help.

You might assume that girls at this age would be more caring and empathic than their male counterparts. However, in general, children display few sex differences in their degree of helping and sharing. For example, when actually in the presence of a crying baby, young boys are just as likely to assist as girls.

Most of us grew up with parents who inadvertently stifled our propensity to reason morally. Your father bellowed, "Don't ask me why, just do it!" When pushed further by you for explanation, he fell back on, "Because I'm your father, and I said so!" But a few of us were fortunate enough to be raised by a mother who amplified her admonitions: "Don't take Robert's toy. That makes him sad. How would you like it if someone took your toy?" She planted empathic seeds.

On an evolutionary level, it makes sense that females and males would have the same *capacity* for empathy. Females guarded the hearth and children while the male foraged for food and turned aside external predators. Both, however, required well-developed antennae to ascertain the intentions of intruders. In modern times, however, while females have been allowed the expression of their empathic, cooperative abilities, men have been discouraged from exercising a propensity that might interfere with their aggressive, competitive drive.

As we move through life, we consider what we want to consider. We can severely constrict our concern and switch off our ability to empathize, even when face-to-face with the tearful eyes of another we have wronged. We can also endlessly stretch our capacity for concern in order to preserve the earth's natural resources for future generations. Yes, we have the ability to be empathic. But we must want to *activate* that ability.

Most of us are fairly adept at "reading" other people, sensing their shifting moods. When we act out of selfish impulses, however, we suspend that facility. We don't want to care about the effect our behavior has on the other because that might produce hesitation, a conflict, an awareness of the unkindness of our actions. Remember that, through everything, we have a profound need to maintain a positive perception of ourselves.

In order to empathize, you must put yourself in the other's shoes. You must imagine what he might be feeling as he is confronted by life's choices and challenges. You must take into consideration his temperament, his proclivities, his way of viewing the world, for all of these will influence his reactions. As you can see, real empathy compels effort.

When you think about another's needs or insecurities, you do not imply an excusing of his behavior. But the more you assume the other's frame of reference and the more you try to understand what makes him tick, the more you humanize him. And the more you humanize him, the more hesitant you will be to judge and feel morally superior. True sensitivity to another requires a genuine commitment to thoughtfulness, fairness, and compassion. Loving humanity is easy. It demands nothing of you. Simply treating each individual with consideration presents a far greater challenge.

Understandably, but regrettably, we find it much more difficult to identify with the stranger than those more familiar and biologically or ethnically closer. In most instances, you are more likely to go out of your way for a relative or friend than a neighbor (regardless of who might be more deserving). You are more likely to extend a hand to someone of your ethnic background than an "outsider" (regardless of who is more deserving). You are more likely to rush to the aid of an acquaintance who collapses in the distance than someone whom you had previously never known.

We all have histories of relationships with loved ones that were mixed with hurt and disappointment. Those old grievances sometimes cause us to snap impatiently and lose perspective. However, especially with blood ties, most of us know, deep down, that we can always count on one another in a pinch. In general, however, the more removed we are, either genetically or emotionally, from another, the less inclined we are to consider him. You are probably more motivated to act sensitively toward your spouse than toward a stranger. But being our best self demands that we approach both with the same considerations. We are all strangers to most people.

Doing the right thing can be a complex matter. You want to do what is fair to you. You want to take into account the needs of others. You want everyone to feel good about the outcome. (Of course, this last wish may be unrealistic.)

However, there are times when our moral sense is obscured. When we observe others acting in a selfish or unjust manner, it lowers our resistance to follow suit. Indeed, our expectations that others will behave in a self-serving manner often provides us with the excuse to "beat him to the punch." Our view of the world as a morally corrupt one diminishes the discomfort we might feel about our own immoral behavior. We experience a perverse excitement on the one hand, and a resigned acceptance, on the other hand, at the moral failings of our leaders because they serve to further excuse our missteps. "If the President of the United States could do that, aren't I entitled to a little slack?" At the very least, we retain our positive self-image by thinking, "Everyone does some things which are not so nice and I'm just a person, too." People were not meant to be perfect, you reassure yourself.

Fortunately, this circular reasoning can move in an uplifting direction as well. I cannot force you to act morally. But my own display of fairness can help you feel safer, as well as inspire you to do the same. Subsequently, seeing you act more justly can breathe more life into my moral inclination.

Presently, you probably act more morally in some situations than others. You probably allow yourself greater sensitivity in some relationships versus others. Understandably, and problematically, we tend to act morally *when it is convenient.*

Acting morally may not always come naturally to you. There have been too many years of anxiety-driven decisions, too many reflexive absolutions casually accepted with, "It doesn't *really* matter." But the mere presence of the natural gift of empathy demands that we utilize and act on that ability in order to truly actualize.

When we want to strengthen a part of our body, we exercise it. I want you to exercise your soul. I want your moral self, your higher self, to attain a strength, a resoluteness, and a clarity that will enable you to make the right choices.

Writing this book has forced me to pause in my daily life. It has prodded me to ask difficult questions of myself. It has allowed me to be more aware of momentary decisions.

Am I being as generous as I can be right now?
Am I treating this stranger with the same consideration that I would a friend?
Should I apologize?
Will I be slower to feel aggrieved even though she has hurt me? Will I consider, with greater compassion and understanding, what might have caused her to act as she did? Will I refrain from retaliating, even though I feel like doing so? Will I be more reluctant to judge her?

Will I make this personal sacrifice so that my community will
   live more harmoniously?
Will I stifle a deserved retort to his ridiculous remarks because
   they would only make him feel even more inadequate?
Will I go out of my way to help her feel good about herself?
Despite my loathing of meetings and organizational structure,
   will I volunteer to serve on that school committee because
   someone has to?
Perhaps he didn't understand the implications of his remarks.
   Perhaps he only intended to help. *Will I give him the benefit
   of the doubt?*

The path I offer you is a challenging one. It may seem so contrary
to what you observe around you. And this contrariness may be frightening. Indeed, a certain courage is required to act fairly with the
knowledge that another may not act fairly in return. You may say
to yourself, "How can I be expected to do what is right when others
simply act out of self-interest? Aren't I being naive? Won't I suffer
when others do not act as compassionately as me?"

But those are your fears paralyzing you. Inner peace, inner
strength, a true sense of righteousness will come from acting fairly,
kindly, and sensitively. Acting morally is in your best interest. When
we act unfairly or insensitively, we not only hurt another, but we
subdue our own natural hunger for justice. We move further away
from an honesty that becomes lost in a web of self-justification. This
is a book about getting beyond excuses. This is a book about doing
what is right regardless of how others behave.

As adults, many of us find ourselves embedded in bureaucracies
or organizational structures in business that demand that we simply
follow prescribed rules of behavior, not question them. Moreover,
we are often told that thinking through decisions is not a part of
our responsibility or job requirement. It is made clear to us that

issues of fairness and compassion are *irrelevant* to success and its attendant rewards.

Traditionally, the analysis of moral conflicts has been the purview of philosophers and theologians. We can no longer afford that luxury. Every one of us must join the discussion in order to activate our higher self. Moral growth does not occur as a result of the blind incorporation of dos and don'ts and subsequent rewards or punishments for adherence to them. As mentioned earlier, the morally intelligent individual knows not only how to behave morally, but how to think morally, as well. Cultivating our moral intelligence, therefore, requires practice in moral-analytical reasoning. To that end, moral reasoning strategies must be learned. One of the best ways to do so is to be presented with unresolved moral dilemmas.

In Section Two, I introduce you to scenarios that require decisions on your part. You will not find yourself grappling with all or even most of these dilemmas in your real life. But my goal is for you to develop a new way of thinking. I want you to practice assuming different perspectives that will help you arrive at a just solution. Let yourself be swept up into these dilemmas so that you care about the choices you make. Give your imagination full rein as you explore the intricacies, the people, and the conflicts. I want you to be able to analyze a complex situation and answer the question, "What's the right thing to do?"

Many predicaments entail complicated, ambiguous, or perplexing factors. There may be several valid points of view and several reasonable courses of action. You will be asked to choose between competing loyalties. You will be required to determine which values supersede others. There may not be an indisputably correct path. Life is complex, and so is morality. But you will learn the right questions to ask in arriving at less than clear-cut resolutions as well. The object is not to settle things with an "answer," but to dive into the process.

Research consistently verifies that our level of moral reasoning regresses as issues become more personal. We think less analytically when self-interest is at stake. My goal is to reverse this process. The closer to home an issue hits, the more deliberate and conscious you must become about your choices. My hope is that the more you exercise your moral self, the more easily it will kick in when confronted with inevitable conflicts in your own world, conflicts that will require you to choose between acting out of fear or acting out of goodness.

I am concerned about my children and your children as well. As fathers and mothers, we have the greatest potential for influencing our child's development. (In fact, we can have more of an effect on their morality than their personality.) When parents do little to encourage discussion of moral issues, a child's moral reasoning abilities will be retarded. Section Three provides moral dilemmas involving children that will hopefully serve as a springboard for that discussion.

You may have self-doubt about your moral strength. "I'm doing the best I can" is a refrain I hear on a daily basis. But as a psychologist, I have been privy to countless individuals overcoming supposed self-limitations. I believe in you and your potential for goodness.

All of us have witnessed individuals who engaged in heroic or mundane acts of moral rectitude. Remember how you admired those individuals. Remember how you were, at least momentarily, inspired by them. And remember that your capacity for fairness is just as great. The actions of the Just speak to us; they speak to our desire to do likewise.

Moral conduct has always fallen short of moral ideals. What is astounding is that the moral ideals of today ask for so little. Sadly, being a more moral person is not even a goal to which we all aspire. No one is morally pure. We all stumble. But we can do better. The key is in the *striving* and the resolve to *activate* our moral self.

SECTION ONE

CHAPTER ONE

The Keys to Morality

I AM IN THE PARKING LOT OF A SHOPPING MALL near my home and observe a car backing up and slightly scraping the automobile parked next to it. A thirtyish-looking man in a dark blue suit emerges from the offending vehicle, takes a business card out of his pocket, scribbles a note on the back, and puts it under the windshield of the damaged Toyota.

The act of honesty warms me, but I am also aware of being a little startled. It is the unexpectedness of it that startles. It is the same feeling I get when I witness an act of generosity ("You asked if I could give ten dollars to your charity? How about twenty?"), observe an act of considerateness ("You look pregnant and tired. Would you like my seat?"), spot an act of kindness between strangers ("You seem pale and about to faint. Can I help you?"), or experience an act of anticipation by another ("Sure, I can give you a ride to the airport. But how are you going to get back?") Simple acts, all of them. But extraordinary in their infrequency.

What motivated these people to act from their higher self, their self that encourages kindness and sensitivity to others?

To act morally, we must feel the thread that binds us to one another. The process must begin early. Psychologists universally emphasize the critical importance of an infant's experiencing a sustained, nurturing, secure attachment to an adult as a necessary precursor to becoming a caring human being.

We can be taught and inspired by the example of those around us. Rewards for moral behavior and punishment for transgressions have only fleeting impact, however. When the incentive is withdrawn, or the fear of retribution is removed, what's to keep us on the right path? Why be good when no one is watching?

Above all, what is required for me to be moral is my ability to truly empathize. I must understand your feelings, thoughts, and needs. I must be able to feel your pain. I must see the world through your eyes. I must feel secure enough in myself to extend my concern to you. I must appreciate you as worthy of my attention, simply and profoundly because you are a human being.

We call them gooks or slopeheads so we can kill them. With a clear conscience. I have to first dehumanize him so I can kill him without compunction. If he has intrinsic worth, how can I pull the trigger? Before I annihilate him, I must be certain he is not at all like me.

Using very different language, Anna Freud suggested that altruistic behavior, on the other hand, springs from the reverse process; that is, I unconsciously view you as similar to me and provide aid and comfort in order to vicariously gratify my own needs. Indeed, on a conscious level, *how can I compassionately understand you if I am not a little like you?*

Cheap Empathy

IF I AM PREOCCUPIED WITH MYSELF, IF I FEEL A FUNDAMENTAL SENSE of deprivation, I can only offer "cheap empathy." A variation of the following encounter is familiar to all of us: You run into a neighbor or acquaintance at the grocery store. Judy asks, "So, how are things going?" Despite knowing that this was simply a polite question and one designed to elicit a reflexive and dishonest "Fine," you feel overwhelmed enough to be honest. "Frank just lost his job. My mother was diagnosed with cancer of the liver last week. It's a rough time." As you unveil your woes, Judy grimaces in concern and nods her head in a sympathetic manner. But for Judy, it's time to continue with her shopping. "I'm sorry to hear it. Let me know if there's anything I can do." Judy and her shopping cart disappear around the next aisle. You are left feeling just as alone in your travails as you were before the contact.

Indeed, Judy may have felt a flicker of distress. But she moves away from it as quickly as possible. She hurriedly departs because she is intent on calming herself.

When I truly empathize with you, I allow your experience to penetrate my psyche. I *share* some of your pain. I don't run from it.

While many women may feign empathy, most men are simply frightened of it. A classic and common example of men's unwillingness to empathize occurs when a wife attempts to speak with her husband about her fears or anxieties. Amanda says: "I'm feeling old. I know I'm only forty-five, but I'm feeling old. Bonnie and Andy don't need me anymore; they're teenagers, they're in their own world. Maybe I did it wrong. Fifteen years ago, I knew I wanted to be home for the kids while they were growing up. I feel too old to start a career. Maybe I made a mistake. What's my life now?" Charley responds: "Maybe you could take up some hobby like tennis."

Men are too frightened to identify with powerlessness, indecision, and anxiety. No wallowing allowed. None of that existential angst crap. Just do something about it. Take a pill. Take a tennis class. The old adage is true: Women want to talk, share, connect, be known, and know the other. Men want to fix it. Men want to avoid the specter of vulnerability.

How Do We Develop Empathy?

A NINE-MONTH-OLD, MARIE, BECOMES ALARMED WHEN SHE SEES HER seven-year-old brother, Todd, crying. But she is not sure who is hurt because she cannot clearly distinguish between herself and her brother. Two months later, Marie observes Todd fall and hurt himself. To reduce her anxiety, Marie sucks her thumb vigorously and buries her head in her mother's lap. She is still unsure of who is really in pain.

A few months later, Marie becomes aware that Todd is, indeed, a separate person. (She has achieved what psychologists term "object permanence.") When Todd falls off his bicycle, Marie understands that, while Todd is injured, she is fine. Her distress is transformed from simple empathy with her injured brother to sympathetic concern for his condition. She now not only wants to calm herself, but she also hopes to relieve Todd's suffering. However, her overwhelming self-centeredness may still cause her to offer something that would soothe her, but not necessarily comfort Todd. Marie may fetch her security blanket for him.

By two or three, Marie will understand that people's needs differ. For the first time, she will make an effort to put herself in the other's place. When Todd is hurt, she will offer him her baseball cards because Todd sleeps with his baseball glove and watches the Dodgers any time he can. By five, Marie even understands that her six-year-old cousin, Harrison, who lives three thousand miles away, is a handicapped child with certain life limitations.

Marie was not only capable of empathizing at a very early age, she was also able to act in a caring fashion. When she was one, she obviously shared, helped, protected, and nurtured *without any necessary prompting or praise.* She "fed," groomed, caressed, and talked to her dolls and stuffed animals.

Marie's two-year-old sister, Samantha, always had a very different kind of temperament. From birth, Samantha was irritable and stubborn. When she observed Todd fall off his bicycle, she was curious about what had happened, but didn't run for her favorite blanket in order to ease his pain. On a couple of occasions, she simply remarked, "Todd was riding too fast. He shouldn't have done that." Individual temperament always affects our sensitivity to others.

Since empathy occupies the heart of morality, we have a stake in fostering it in all our children. How can we do that?

Let your child fail. We can love, encourage, and reassure our children, but we can't always protect them. Nor should we. When we shield our children from life's disappointments and cruelty, they will be ill-equipped to move through the world on their own. Sensitivity to the needs and feelings of others can only occur if a child has the normal range of upsetting experiences.

Provide your child contact with the less fortunate. Take your child to a soup kitchen or a homeless shelter. By providing aid to the needy, he can begin to empathize with those who have problems unlike his own.

Let your child help. Children growing up in cultures where they are assigned responsibility for taking care of siblings and other relatives (such as Kenya, Mexico, and the Philippines) are more likely to exhibit a range of helping behaviors than children who grow up in societies without those expectations (like the United States).

Take any opportunity to encourage your child to place himself in another's shoes. Help him try on different perspectives. Stretch his imaginative capacities. ("What do you think it would feel like to be Danny, right now?" "How do you think you would feel if your best friend decided to be best friends with another girl?")

Instead of trying to instill morality by teaching rules, help your child understand the emotional consequences of his behavior for others. When your child does something that is selfish, cruel, thoughtless, or contrary to what you had ordered, your tendency is to spontaneously explode: "How could you do that? Haven't I told you——!" Part of your anger stems from a perception that your child has defied you, and you take his defiance personally ("I'll show you who's boss!"). You told him the first time, the second time, and even the third. You yell because you feel ineffectual. You scold out of a sense of desperation. You punish in order to "teach him a lesson."

But when you simply punish or express your disappointment, your child will focus on his resentment, anxiety, and the negative impact on his life, rather than on the sensibilities of those he has wronged.

Help your child feel good about himself. When we are feeling insecure, deprived, or unwanted, we become preoccupied with our own supposed deficiencies. Shifting our focus outward so we can empathize with another requires that we feel secure about our place in the world. I must feel loved before I can extend love to others.

We can foster self-esteem in our children on a daily basis. Try this brief assessment. Answer True or False to the following:

I hug my child a lot.

I frequently tell my child "I love you."

When my child says "I hate you," I don't simply react. Instead, I try to understand why he is so angry.

When my child talks to me, I stop what I'm doing and listen to him.

I give my child a lot more praise than criticism.

I am patient with my child.

I am able to control the frustrations in other parts of my life and not take them out on my child.

I help my child verbalize his feelings.

I am conscious of telling my child what I like about him.

Were you able to answer "True" to most of the statements?

Stretching Our Empathy

MARTIN SOLOMON, A THIRTY-EIGHT-YEAR-OLD ORTHOPEDIC SURGEON, has lost everything—his home, his practice, his wife, and his children. He is a compulsive gambler. After twenty years of denial, he has concluded it is time to look at himself. He wonders if I can help him. "Can you possibly know what it's like?" he asks desperately.

Fiona Walsh, a twenty-nine-year-old associate in a public relations firm, was the victim of incest. From the ages of nine until twelve, her father crept into her darkened bedroom on a nightly basis, fondling her in the name of love. Fiona's inability to allow physical or emotional intimacy drove her to psychotherapy. She is uncertain about whether a man, and one who had never experienced the ultimate violation, can relate to her. "I don't know if you can imagine what it felt like," she whispers despairingly.

Indeed, I could not possibly have experienced the range of problems that have been presented to me over my twenty-five years of practicing as a clinical psychologist. No, I have never been a compulsive gambler. But I have known the feeling of being out of control, hurtling down a self-destructive path, and thinking, "I just can't help myself. I *don't want* to help myself." I have known the shame and weakness of promising myself and others that I will never do that again, and promptly breaking my word because of a seemingly uncontrollable impulse. I have known the rush of excitement and the defeating confrontation with failure. I have known the sadness of loss.

No, I was never molested as a child. But I have known the pain of betrayal by someone I had implicitly trusted. I have experienced the powerlessness of being physically controlled by a stronger presence. I have grappled with confusion and anxiety when I have not been clear about whose fault it was when something horrible happened.

As I said in the Introduction, genuine empathy requires effort. When someone speaks of an incident that you have never known, think of the feelings that might accompany such an episode. Then, remember an event in your own life that produced similar reactions. We understand another best when we can relate a personal circumstance that seems parallel. We also feel closer to those we perceive to be similar to ourselves.

Because we are cut of the same human cloth, we can empathize with the experience of others despite their apparent foreign nature. Few of us go through life without brushing against hopelessness, fear, rejection, betrayal, powerlessness, insensitivity, shame, or despair. Most of us have had at least a fleeting thought of suicide somewhere along the line. No, it is not difficult to empathize with another whose problem seems so different from any we have encountered. None of us has had the *exact* experience of another. Nevertheless, we can empathize if we stretch our imagination to find our human common ground.

When We Don't Empathize

TWENTY-THREE-YEAR-OLD BERNARD WATSON IS A BURGLAR. HE ROBS houses for a living. When told that he had stolen an irreplaceable gold pocket watch that had been passed down through five generations to his victim, he offered: "I can't feel bad for him. Tough luck. He shoulda had his house locked better. He shoulda had an alarm system that really worked. He made it so easy, it was pathetic."

This is how twenty-one-year-old Wiley Thornton explained why he had raped three teenage girls the previous year. "Doc, you should have seen what they were wearing. Those tight sweaters, those miniskirts. They're showing off what they got. Why do you think they were struttin' their stuff? They want it. They can't come right out and say it 'cause girls aren't supposed to want it. But they do. You can't tell me otherwise. So, you see, it was what they call 'consensual.' They wanted it as bad as I did."

Bernard Watson and Wiley Thornton have never developed the concept of a "responsible self." That is, they do not feel responsible for the consequences of their actions for others. Even you and I suppress any sympathy for the victim when we inflict pain. And, because we must maintain a positive self-image, we further hold the victim responsible for his ill-fortune. When you cheat me out of something that is rightfully mine, you remind yourself of how I treated you unfairly two months ago.

For many of us, the activation of our empathic potential is often superficial and arbitrary. You may have noticed that:

You are more likely to empathize when you like the other person.

You are more likely to empathize when you want the other person to like you.

You are more likely to empathize when you view the other person's reaction as legitimate. You extend much less sympathy and understanding for those you blithely label "neurotic."

You are more likely to empathize when you perceive the other person's needs to be similar to your own.

You are more likely to empathize with the other person if you have experienced similar difficulties.

You are more likely to empathize when you want to influence or manipulate another.

Yes, we tend to pick and choose, at our convenience.

What's Fair?

THE SENTIMENT IS ABSOLUTELY PRIMITIVE. EVEN THE VERY YOUNG feel the sting of injustice. Children have acute moral sensibilities. We have all witnessed a child's spontaneous expressions of hurt and anger when he perceives injustice has been done to him. My five-year-old, Nathan, rushes into the kitchen excitedly to show me the Super-Soaker squirt gun his mother bought him that day. He is beaming. As he enters the room, he spies his sister eating chocolate-chip ice cream and reflexively asks, "Can I have some ice cream, too?" I tell him, "No, you had a tummyache this afternoon." Instant wailing. He stomps out of the kitchen, crying uncontrollably, his new toy forgotten on the kitchen table.

Whether you are five or forty-five, you have exclaimed, "That's not fair!" In our bleaker moments, the singular easily becomes the universal: "Life's not fair!" But how do we learn what's fair?

As young as two years of age, children play and learn about morality. As children give and receive toys, turns, and favors, they encounter others' expectations of justice. The incentive to abide by rules of fairness is a powerful one: Children want to play with other children. Children want friends, and sharing is the key to social acceptance.

At the neighborhood playground, my then fourteen-month-old son, Nathan, was getting bored playing by himself in the sand. He took his firetruck, shovel, and pail over to another boy, stretched out his hand, and mutely offered his possessions to share. Nathan had already learned the admission ticket to friendship.

Parents may prod, order, bribe, or cajole, but a child's primary reason for cooperative play is his desire for acceptance. Most of the time when children play, adults are not around. It is through negotiation and acts of generosity that we learn our first lessons about fairness. We also learn that getting along often means making deals, and sometimes, it requires simply giving in. As a child plays with others, he experiences relationships of mutual respect. He sees his playmate, even his opponent, as someone like himself.

Prior to his extensive exposure with peers at play, a child only has respect for adult authority. Slowly, with his friends, he learns that he must extend that respect to all. Rules for play evolve by consensual agreement with the other boys and girls. Eventually, the child realizes that fairness is a principle that applies in every relationship. It is through games and play, not parental edicts, that we learn about fairness. Our mature notions of morality are born in these early critical interactions. We learn that justice is based on reciprocal consideration, and not on the use of superior power.

Our idea of justice evolves quickly. During preschool, a child shares when and with whom he wants. Sharing need not extend, for example, beyond a favorite friend or preferred group (such as boys or girls). But by the fourth year, a child has internalized the notion that he has an obligation to share his possessions with others on occasion. (Note: He may not be quite as generous with his favorite toys as with other property.) By the time he begins elementary school, a child has firmly learned three criteria for fairness: equality (ensuring that everyone is treated identically), merit (extra rewards are due for exceptional performance), and benevolence (those with special handicaps should be given special consideration).

Over the course of many years and many thousands of encounters with his peers, a child's understanding of justice deepens. This understanding can manifest considerable flexibility as one applies different principles of justice to fit one's interests. For example, the oldest child may decide she gets the biggest slice of cake because she is the oldest, but not necessarily more household chores than her younger siblings. The important point, however, is that the child knows he must appeal to some standard of justice in order to advance his position and resolve competing claims.

Sibling relationships provide other powerful lessons in fairness. My twelve-year-old daughter, Rachel, yells: "You never criticize Sarah. Why do you always pick on me?" My eight-year-old daughter, Sarah, screams: "Why do I have to share everything with Nathan?" My five-year-old son, Nathan, cries: "Why do I have to let her play with my new toy? She doesn't let me play with hers!" My children are fighting for their rights, asking questions designed to test the parameters of justice and always searching for telltale answers to "Who do Mommy and Daddy love the most?"

While we no longer stomp our feet in outrage, the sense of "That's not fair!" stays with us into adulthood. At forty-nine, I am still assessing if I have gotten my fair share. I have smart, sensitive, healthy children. I have a warm, supportive, loving wife. I have work that allows me to feel productive and useful. I can afford a nice lifestyle. So, why do I find myself thinking:

Why is that gorgeous woman with him and not me?
Why can't I have a job as interesting as his?
Why don't I make as much money as he does?

"That's not fair!" is what I feel. I feel it because my primitive sense of justice invokes the lesson I learned when my innocence was in full bloom: He doesn't deserve it more than I do. In my weaker moments, my moments of frustration and perceived deprivation, that five-year-old boy lurking in a corner of my forty-nine-year-old body cries out, "It's not fair!" Unfortunately, we tend to fix our gaze on those who seem to have more than we do and not less. And at those times, of course, we fail to appreciate our own good fortune.

Guilt Can Help

SINCE THE 1960s, GUILT HAS GOTTEN A BAD RAP, AND IT IS MY PROFESSION that is, perhaps, mostly to blame. Caught up in the spirit of antipathy to authority, many psychotherapists declared *should* a dirty word. *Should* inhibited expression and tied the person to dictates emanating from outside of oneself. We were exhorted to "Be true to yourself." *Self* became the operative word.

To be sure, guilt is often unwarranted. In 1974, my father died of a massive heart attack at the age of fifty-seven. Two weeks before he died, I flew in to New York to visit him and my mother (they were divorced at the time). He looked bad to me. His normally cherub face was gray, almost ashen. Usually physically robust and vigorous, he uncharacteristically admitted to me, "I haven't felt good lately."

"Have you been to the doctor?" I asked.

"Yeah, I saw Dr. Bitterman," he answered. "He said I'm okay."

And, with all the self-absorption of a twenty-five-year-old, I dropped it.

After I received the fateful call, I berated myself. I should have pushed more. I should have insisted he see another physician. Dr. Bitterman had been our family doctor for twelve years when we lived in Brooklyn. His idea of a complete physical was to weigh you, put a thermometer in your mouth, and measure your blood pressure. The visit would last an average of five minutes. I chastened myself for years. When I would think about what I had not done, shivers would pulsate down my spine. I was so self-centered. Even when it came to the life of my father.

Guilt is not helpful when it stems from things that are truly not your fault.

Today, Abraham Pasternak is a seventy-four-year-old retired businessman, living in an affluent suburb of Detroit. But fifty-three years ago, he lived in a different place. "I arrived at Auschwitz on a transport from Hungary with my parents and four brothers. That very same day there were so many things that happened to us. We really couldn't sort them out, and I'm still trying to sort out that day. . . . My parents were sent to the left [to their death] and me and my two older brothers and a younger brother were sent to the right. I told my little kid brother, I said to him, 'Solly, gey tsu Tate un Mame' [Go to Poppa and Momma]. And like a little kid, he followed. . . . He did. Little did I know that I sent him to the crematorium. I am . . . I feel like I killed him. My [older] brother, who lives now in New York . . . every time when we see each other he talks about him. And he says, 'No, I am responsible, because I said that same thing to you. And it's been bothering me too.' I've been thinking whether he reached my mother and father, and that he *did* reach my mother and father. He probably told them, he said, '*Avrum hot mir gezugt, dos ikh zol geyn mit aykh* [Abraham said I should go with you].' I wonder what my mother and father were thinking, especially when they were all . . . when they all went into the crematorium [that is, the gas chamber]. I can't get it out of my head. It hurts me, it bothers me, and I don't know what to do."

Obviously, it is not simply life and death issues that generate unwarranted guilt. A few years ago, my friend Stan recommended that I buy a stock. He had a "hot tip." Stan had already bought several thousand shares and suggested it would be good if I got in on the run-up. Although I don't play the stock market, I couldn't resist the opportunity. After a very brief positive move, the stock crashed, and I lost everything. "I feel terrible about having gotten you into it," Stan has reiterated on several occasions. My response has always been, "Don't be ridiculous. I'm a big boy. I chose to take the risk. Nobody forced me to."

Guilt is not helpful when the hurtful act was not foreseeable.

One day, a colleague popped her head into my office. "Aaron, do you have a minute?"

"Sure," I replied.

"I just ran into Bob Grant, and he was upset," she continued. "He said you had scheduled a meeting with him a long time ago for yesterday, and when he came by, you barely acknowledged him and immediately rushed out of your office. He's very anxious about applying to graduate school and really wanted to talk with you about it."

My heart sank. Yesterday had been one of those pressure-filled nightmares. I had forgotten to closely check my calendar, was preoccupied with ten things I had to get done in the next hour after Bob's arrival, and had not even taken the time to inquire patiently why he was standing at my office door. I felt awful, but not guilty.

Guilt is not helpful when you have unintentionally hurt or neglected someone. (However, an apology is in order.)

Eighteen years ago, Margaret, then twenty-four, and Jim, twenty-six, were in love and living together. Margaret was immersed in her second year of a sociology doctoral program, and Jim was a local television reporter. After only two years on the job, Jim received an offer to anchor a newscast in a larger market, and Margaret's life began a predictable trajectory: "I quit the doctoral program even though I loved it. The last twenty or so years I've been following Jim from station to station and city to city. Every time I would start to build a life for myself, we had to move. When the kids got older and were in school, several interesting job offers came my way. I thought about them, but Jim said we didn't need the additional income and he would prefer it if I was home when the kids got back from school every day. It sounded right to me. . . . So much of my life has been about just taking care of everyone else.

"I never questioned having to uproot myself so much for Jim's work. His career always came first. . . . One time, I even started a great job at an advertising agency. I was so excited. I felt alive again, challenged. And then, Jim got a better offer. He was sure I could find something I liked in Los Angeles, but this was a career move that would only come along once in a lifetime, he said. He was always so persuasive."

Margaret's life of deferring to others and feeling guilty about having needs of her own began early. With both of her parents full-time attorneys, and as the oldest of three children, she was expected to be the dutiful daughter and tend to her younger sister and brother. When Margaret was fifteen, her mother suffered a disabling stroke. During those years that should have been filled with friendships, after-school activities, and parties, Margaret was forced to stay close to home. Her impulse to insist, "But what about *my* life?" was further squelched by the sight of her mother's contorted face and body. It's not that Margaret didn't receive recognition for her sacrifices. Her parents always bragged about what a good, helpful girl she was, about how Margaret "always put others first." Unfortunately, while Margaret was being responsible and generous, she lost herself. She lost her capacity to articulate her needs. She lost her sense of entitlement.

Guilt is not helpful when it stifles your ability to assert, "I'm a person, too."

Too often, people go overboard in their self-punishment. But guilt can be helpful as well.

The mere fact that you can feel guilt is testimony to your ability to empathize. One must first realize what one did (or failed to do) to another in order to feel guilt's pangs. Good guilt can provide a moral compass. I know I'll feel guilty saying "no" to a neighbor who needs my assistance to stem the tide of his plumbing disaster, even though helping him will mean missing my cherished weekly basketball game. I know I'll feel guilty saying "no" to my sick neighbor's request to pick up her child from school, simply because it would be inconvenient. I know I'll feel guilty if I make up some excuse to my daughter about why I can't take her and her friends to the movies this weekend. Furthermore, the anticipation of guilt can help you control impulses that would be hurtful to others. Despite a strong, mutual attraction, I won't go out with the woman who broke off the love affair with my friend because it would be too painful for him to bear.

Good guilt can allow the pain of your acknowledged mistake to prompt your resolve to do better. (You know how much you hurt your daughter when you didn't go to her last class play, so you'll be sure to go to the one this coming week. You didn't understand how much Valentine's Day meant to your wife, so you promise yourself to make up for your negligence and buy her a nice gift next year.) On the other hand, when you provide ready excuses for your actions ("She won't even notice," "I couldn't help myself," "He had it coming," "It's not a big deal"), you not only fail to take responsibility for them, but you avoid even the recognition that you screwed up.

For most of us, guilt is superficial and manageable. It usually lasts for just a few moments, perhaps for an hour or two. If our behavior was truly egregious, maybe a day. But, as I said in the Introduction, we reflexively justify our immoral behavior, or simply forget about it and move on.

We sometimes attempt to induce guilt in another in order to get him to do what's right. Coming from the outside, it is a tool that must be used carefully and sparingly. Usually, we get angry at a person who makes us feel guilty. Any desire to correct our behavior drowns in a sea of resentment ("Don't tell me what to do!"). My guilt induction can paralyze you, as your anger battles with your desire to act correctively. Nevertheless, it is my place to tell you, "I think you acted really insensitively toward Ron. You might want to offer an apology."

Unfortunately, we often use guilt to further our self-centered interests, without concern for the pain it might cause another. Parents do that a lot to their children. "Why is it that a mother can take care of three children, but three children can't take care of one mother?" our aging parent who lives in a nursing home wants to know.

A mother buys her adult son a blue sweater and a yellow sweater for his birthday. "Why don't you wear one tonight when you go out?" she suggests. As he is about to leave to pick up his date, his mother notices that he is wearing the blue sweater. "What's the matter?" she says. "You didn't like the yellow sweater?"

While we must be judicious in our use of guilt induction, we must recoil from any act that might produce *shame*. The Talmud (a body of Jewish law and interpretations discussed by rabbinic sages and later recorded in the fourth and fifth centuries as sacred teachings) warns that humiliating someone is the equivalent of murder. In one section it says, "The person who makes someone else ashamed in the presence of others is as if the person has shed blood." Shame cuts much more deeply than guilt. Listen to the exquisitely shaded contrast between guilt and shame provided by the noted psychiatrist and psychoanalyst James Gilligan:

By guilt I mean the feeling of having committed a sin, a crime, an evil, or an injustice; the feeling of culpability; the feeling of obligation; the feeling of being dangerous or harmful to others; and the feeling of needing expiation and deserving punishment.

By shame I mean the feelings of inferiority, humiliation, embarrassment, inadequacy, incompetence, weakness, dishonor, disgrace, "loss of face"; the feeling of being vulnerable to, or actually experiencing . . . insult, derision, scorn, rejection . . . ; the feeling of not being able to "take care of" oneself.

I feel guilt when I have failed to do what is right. When I feel guilt, I also experience some apprehension about your potential resentment or indignation. My guilt implies that I would like to do better. There is no joy in believing that I have failed my better self.

When I feel shame, however, my *character* is deemed defective. Shame raises questions of what kind of person I am. I anticipate your contempt and ridicule. I have shown myself unworthy of your association.

Shame requires witnesses (or the imagined presence of others). When I was in the sixth grade, I was popular with the girls, and this galled my classmate Joey Ambrosio. As a result, Joey took it upon himself to make my life miserable. He would delight in any occasion to taunt me, bump me, or threaten me. One day after school, I was walking home with my girlfriend, Helene Lightman, when Joey, accompanied by two of his friends, ambushed me. Shrieking with delight, Joey punched me, kicked me, and then just sat on me. I was a skinny kid, and Joey must have had fifty percent more body weight than I did. I felt frightened and powerless. But glimpsing Helene's shocked face produced the most acute pain, the pain of humiliation. For literally decades after, I had vivid nightmares of that afternoon scene on Avenue L and East 26th Street.

Shame is difficult to dispel. One feels compelled to provide proof (to oneself and/or others) of a fundamental character weakness that

has been corrected. But the means to erasing guilt in a moral manner are readily available. Guilt is the prod that reminds us something
needs to be repaired. Reparation can range from providing sincere
apology to an act that counterbalances the original offense, but it
must be public. Simply resolving to oneself to "do better" is not
sufficient.

One day at the park, I observed a boy of about five accidentally
knock down a girl of perhaps three while he was on a swing. He
stopped, offered the girl his swing, and gave her a long ride, while
pushing her gently. After I inadvertently snubbed Bob Grant, I an-
nounced in my undergraduate class that I would be setting aside an
extra two hours of advising time specifically for those who had questions concerning graduate study. I also apologized to Bob for my
preoccupation and failure of memory.

It is tragic when sins committed by fathers have guilty reverbera-
tions through subsequent generations. We should feel responsible
for our own behavior, but not another's actions, even if that person
is tied to us by blood. Nevertheless, I have come across examples
of how guilt may stimulate later altruism beyond the immediate
reparation to a particular victim. I remember three Germans, all in
their mid-twenties, all born after the Nazi era, whom I encountered
over the past decade.

I shared a train compartment with Alex as we hurtled from Mu-
nich to Frankfurt. He had recently returned from a year of volunteer
service in a remote, destitute village in Central Africa. Suzanne was
a nurse whom I met at a conference on genocide held in Brussels.
Just two nights previous, she had left Bosnia, where she had volunteered her efforts to work with Muslim rape victims of Serbian soldiers. On a sweltering August afternoon, I ate a hearty lunch with
Arno in the dining room of a kibbutz, where he had come to offer
the sweat of his brow in order to help rebuild the Jewish homeland.
All three of these idealistic Germans informed me that they felt an
obligation to undo the sins of their grandfathers and grandmothers.

Morality in Our Genes

BOTH FREUDIANS AND BEHAVIORISTS HAVE ASSERTED THAT ACTING morally requires the suppression of our natural tendencies. Conscience, they believe, simply represents the internalizing of external constraints. However, it is apparent that the rudiments of moral action evidence themselves long before language or reasoning abilities mature. Researchers have amassed large numbers of examples of friendliness, spontaneous sharing, sympathy, and compassion among very young children.

A little girl, whose parents are away on vacation for two weeks, visits a twenty-month-old boy. As she is about to leave, she cries about her parents' absence. A sad look appears on the boy's face, and then he offers her his beloved teddy bear to take home. Although his parents remind him that he will miss the bear very much, the boy insists that his girlfriend take it. In another instance, a mother scolds her three-year-old's younger brother and is told by her toddler, "Alan's only a baby."

Volumes could be filled with such observations by social scientists. But the point is that they all suggest an inherent resonance in the very young person to the troubles of others. And, as adults, who would not *reflexively* dive for a child teetering on the edge of a cliff?

Some cynics have argued that we help others in order to satisfy egoistic needs. In other words, we extend ourselves primarily because it makes us feel magnanimous to do so. Fortunately, many are not motivated by the anticipated pat on the back.

Jim Wiley, a thirty-four-year-old automobile mechanic, rushed into a burning home in an inner-city neighborhood when he heard the screams of those trapped inside. He eventually emerged safely from the conflagration with a mother and her twin eight-year-old daughters. Don Holmes, a thirty-one-year-old pipe fitter, was driving down a country road when he witnessed a car plunge over the side into a swiftly moving river. He slammed on his brakes and dove into the icy waters to help the family being swept away by the current. Although their heroic forays occurred two thousand miles apart, both men were asked by news reporters, "Why did you risk your own life to save these people?" Their response was a shrug that came from deep within: "Because that's what I *had* to do."

You have been told to go easier on yourself. You have been cautioned not to set very high standards of conduct, lest you feel disappointment at your failure to meet them. You have been reassured that you are fine the way you are.

I don't want you to relax. I want to shake you a bit. I am not suggesting that you commit acts of extraordinary heroism or bravery. But I want you to travel through life with your higher self in full throttle.

Am I good enough? No. Are you good enough? Probably not. Do I deserve to be treated considerately and fairly? Of course. Am I good enough so that I can walk around with a sense of worth and dignity? Definitely. But am I good *enough?* Hardly. I need to be challenged. And so do you.

A *few challenges:*
Will you resolve to activate your better self this coming week?
Will you engage in one act of generosity?
Will you engage in one act of kindness to a stranger?
Will you anticipate a need of someone close to you and offer to fill it?

CHAPTER TWO

Do We Need God in Order to Do the Right Thing?

WE CAN DO WHAT'S RIGHT BECAUSE WE WANT to follow the rules. We can do what's right because we want to consider the consequences of our behavior for others so they will do likewise. We can do what's right because of our sense of fairness. We can do what's right because we want to be a good person. We can do what's right so that others will love us. Or, we can do what's right because God tells us to.

Mostly, we believe in God because we feel vulnerable, and because we crave order. I recently lectured to a group of divinity students about the many Holocaust survivors who, understandably, lost their faith as a result of what they witnessed and endured. Wasn't God supposed to protect the innocent and strike down the guilty? During an interview for my book *The Aftermath*, one survivor told me:

> This [belief in God] I have a big fight in my soul. I would say . . . I don't know how to express myself . . . I would say I don't really believe there is something like God. If there would

be a God, if God is supposed to be so merciful, how could He let children be murdered? My six-year-old brother was killed. One and a half million Jewish children were killed. How could He? Or God is deaf. People pray and pray and pray and He doesn't hear them. Maybe He needs a hearing aid.

"Well, then, what can I say to that congregant?" I was earnestly asked. "If you want, you can give him the standard two-minute explanation about how the Holocaust was perpetrated by man, not God, that God gave man free will and the potential to do good or evil, and the rest of how we attempt to reconcile God and cruelty. But more important is to point out that we don't do God any big favor by believing in Him. *We believe in God because of what that belief does for us.* We choose God because He gives us hope and guidance.

Religion in most early cultures was relatively uninterested in moral behavior between individuals. Your fealty to a god took precedence over how you treated your neighbor. It was demonstrated by the offerings that you made in order to propitiate him or her and forestall misfortune. However, thirty-two hundred years ago, divine law was given to Moses after he led the ancient Jews out of Egypt, and a new concept of devotion was born. Clearly, God's greatest emphases were justice, righteousness, and compassion, with particular concern for the poor and needy.

The Jewish people emphasized judgment, but judgment focused on behavior in this world *as an end to itself.* You weren't expected to act kindly and considerately because that would be your ticket to heaven. You were to act morally because God cared most about how you treated your fellow man. You and God were *partners* in creating a better world. An Eastern European spiritual leader of the nineteenth century taught: If someone comes to you for assistance and you say to him, "God will help you," you become a disloyal servant of God. You have to understand that God has sent you to aid the needy and not refer him back to God. Rabbi Levi Yitzchak of Berditchev told his followers: You can determine whether some- one really loves God by seeing whether he or she loves other people. Both sages emphasized that we are enjoined to alleviate the suffering of our neighbors and make this world a better place for all.

The Judeo-Christian tradition distinguishes Ritual Laws (those per- taining to the relationship between man and God) and Ethical Laws (those affecting human to human relationships). But in our everyday world, when we ask, "Is Robert religious?" we usually mean, Is he ritually observant? That is, Does he go to church every Sunday? Does he tithe? Does he faithfully enter the Confessional? Does he obey the kosher dietary provisions?

"Being religious" means different things to different people. Just as there is no necessary relationship between intelligence and moral- ity, there is no inevitable connection between degree of religiosity and sensitivity to others. "Religious" people steal, commit adultery, and gos- sip. But they find a way to rationalize and compartmentalize their behavior in order to maintain their "religious" self-image. ("That has nothing to do with my belief in God," they say, or "My evil inclina- tion took over momentarily.")

We often obey Ritual Laws in an attempt to quell our anxieties. If I do X, than God will love me and protect me, we tell ourselves. To be sure, Ritual Laws can have tremendous value. They remind us of who we are and our relation to God. They provide discipline by obliging us to perform acts, even when we may not feel like doing so. Assembling with fellow congregants makes me aware of duties beyond myself. When I hear a religious leader speak about the less fortunate, it is a reminder that I owe, that I must live in relation to others.

The mere act of praying together is comforting. We sense the presence of others and a common aspiration. We are reassured of our beliefs because we are surrounded by others whose faith reflects our own. We feel a connection not only to the Divine, but more importantly, to our brothers and sisters. We pray to energize ourselves, to strengthen our resolve, to remind us that there is more than self. Prayer is not about asking God to perform magic. Prayer must prod us (not God) to act.

Like prayer, many rituals have nonritualistic consequences. For example, when I am commanded to Keep the Sabbath Holy, this ritual observance allows me more time to spend with my family, and shifts my focus from material matters to spiritual ones. It forces me to cease my strivings and appreciate what I already have. When I keep *any* imposed ritual, I am reminded that I have obligations beyond my personal desires.

It is those who are only ritually religious who give religion a bad name. Unfortunately, for many, going to church every Sunday or synagogue every Saturday does not provide sufficient armor to inhibit unseemly behavior outside of the sanctuary. But of course, the hypocrisy of the ritually religious rankles most. And we often point to those hypocrites to justify our disavowal of God (as if it were His fault). "I'm not religious, but I'm a spiritual person," is the reaction of many who walked away because they perceived hollowness in sanctimony.

At its best, religious canon not only provides moral guidance, it also attempts to grapple with moral dilemmas. Religiously conservative ideologues adhere to the doctrine of the Establishment and its authorities in resolving these dilemmas, whereas more liberal brands of religion emphasize the need for an individual to arrive at his own sense of how competing interests can be fairly balanced. For the most part, however, theologians use the content of revealed texts as their moral guidepost.

It is my impression that pulpit clergymen tend to differ from prelates far removed from the daily struggle of resolving inconsistencies between doctrine and the untidiness of life as it is lived. Rabbi Harold Schulweis, the spiritual leader of Valley Beth Shalom, is clear about the place of his heart when law collides with real people.

"I used to base my arguments for the acceptance of homosexuals by pointing to biblical chapter and verse or halacha [codified Jewish law]. But I realize that the more fundamental issue is compassion. When I sit across from a couple of sweet, sensitive, *religious* men, who describe to me the humiliation, ridicule, and rejection they have been subjected to, it is my *compassion* which is stirred."

Later on in our conversation, Rabbi Schulweis spoke further of the need for compassion. "The Bible is *preoccupied* with supporting the weaker vessels of our society. It's always referring to the widow, the orphan, or the stranger. . . . It is clear to me that God is foremost a God of compassion much more than He is a God of power and law."

In early 1997, a statement emanating from the Vatican's Pontifical Council for the Family and issued by the offices of His Holiness, John Paul II, brought the latest message for Catholics who divorced: no sex in any new relationship, even a new marriage. Implying his desire to see greater compassion wed to church doctrine, Father Thomas Rausch, chairman of the theology department at Loyola Marymount University in Los Angeles, noted: "In one sense, it's nothing new. The statement upholds the position of the Vatican on the sacredness of marriage. If anything is surprising, it is that it so simply, baldly restates the position, *without sensitivity to remarried Catholics who do not have annulment* [my emphasis]."

The Enlightenment of the eighteenth century extolled the virtues of our rational nature. Man no longer needed to affirm his morality by reference to divine wish. He could resolve competing claims by invoking moral *reasoning* and its ensuing principles. Man would act morally, the philosophers wrote, because it was in his rational interests to do so.

There has always been a tension between faith and reason. For many, it is difficult to believe in the existence of what one can't taste, smell, hear, or see. For others, the cruelty and unfairness of human existence imply the lack of divine order.

But reason and belief need not be at war with one another. Buddha believed that it was *through* our generosities and kindness that we would achieve insight into the divine: "First live in a compassionate way and then you will know." In the thirteenth century, St. Thomas Aquinas taught that God gave man reason so he could recognize his obligations in life. For Aquinas, the moral act was a sign of the close way in which man is able to participate in God's plan. Almost eight hundred years later, in *How Good Do We Have to Be*, Rabbi Harold Kushner wrote: "It is God's caring that invests our moral choices with cosmic significance."

"Because man was created in God's image, he must be treated with dignity," Rabbi Daniel Gordis, a Dean at the University of Judaism, told me, as we sat and spoke in his campus office on a rainy December morning. (I remember the context well because when I entered his office, Rabbi Gordis was speaking on the telephone with his wife about a leak in his roof that was wreaking havoc on his home. I was struck by how calm he was while they discussed calling roofers to come as quickly as possible. Before I left that morning, I said, "I hope your roof issue gets straightened out." He responded, "That should be my biggest problem in life." It was another lesson in what's really worth getting upset about.) Created in God's image, man, therefore, is a sacred creature, one who *mandates* our concern.

Recognizing that faith may become too abstract, Rabbi Gordis uses his imagination to keep him on the right path. "I live as though God is always looking over my shoulder." Rabbi Gordis is a man without doubts about God's existence. For those of us with more tenuous faith, his visualization can provide needed guidance: Live your life as if God is looking over your shoulder. (In *The Art of the Impossible*, Vaclav Havel, playwright, philosopher, and the President of the Czech Republic after the Velvet Revolution in 1989, urges an analogous use of illusion: "None of us—as an individual—can save the world as a whole, but . . . each of us must behave as though it were in his power to do so.")

We hold clergymen and clergywomen to an even higher standard, so I asked all those I interviewed in the course of writing this book, "How do you cope with *your* immoral impulses?" The Reverend Cecil Murray of the First African Methodist Episcopal Church also looks to a greater power in order to strengthen his resolve. "You *will* yourself to say 'yes' to something higher than a 'yes' to you." Reverend Murray then spoke about his keen awareness of more encompassing obligations. "Is there something bigger than your appetite? You don't steal from the church box because it's your community. You don't lust after someone's daughter because you have a commitment to others." Whether it be for God or for community, Reverend Murray tames his self-centered impulses by adopting a wider perspective.

I entered the lobby of the Archdiocese headquarters and told the receptionist that I was there to see Father Coiro. "He's in the cafeteria, right there, across the hall. He's the big one with the brown uniform." A man in brown ecclesiastic robes who fit that description was standing in line to pay for lunch. I introduced myself to the Franciscan friar, and we proceeded to have a far-ranging conversation over the next ninety minutes.

At one point, we were speaking about relationships and sexuality. I recounted an episode in my own life that occurred after the publication of one of my previous books: I had just written *Teenage Sexuality*, and I received a message from the dean of a local Catholic high school who had read the book. He was calling to invite me to speak at the next PTA meeting. I was somewhat stunned. Secular high schools were not beating down my door because, at the time, they considered the topic to be too incendiary.

The dean introduced me to the audience, and in the course of my remarks I spoke about masturbation, as it was, by far, the most common sexual practice among teens. I said that, as a psychologist and not a theologian, I could see several benefits to masturbation for young people. It can relieve some of their sexual tension and, perhaps, keep them out of sexual relationships before they are ready for them. Also, I pointed out that research and clinical evidence clearly indicate that females who learn to masturbate to orgasm are much more likely to be orgasmic once they start having relations with a partner. From my point of view, the only harm from masturbation for these kids occurs when they experience accompanying guilt and anxiety, as too many do.

When my lecture was over, the priest asked if there were any questions or comments from the parents. A man in the front row immediately shot up his hand. "Well, Father, what do you think about this masturbation business? Do you agree with Dr. Hass?" The priest responded, "Our kids have enough to worry about. Let's not give them one more thing to be concerned with." First, there is compassion.

"He was right," Father Coiro responded, jumping in. "I live and teach at a parochial high school for boys. It comes up all the time during confession. I tell the kids, 'Don't beat yourself up about it. *Use* God. He's there to help you when you fall.' " Just as Rabbi Gordis did when he invoked the image of God looking over his shoulder, Father Coiro was teaching his students that remembering God can help keep you on track. God is by your side, and He's rooting for you. The Reverend Billy Graham has often said, "I just want to lobby for God." (And Bishop Fulton J. Sheen once remarked, "An atheist is a man who has no invisible means of support.")

Most of us can use some moral bolstering. One of the great theologians of this century, Professor Abraham Joshua Heschel, once gave a lecture on the relationship between religion and ethics at the University of California. When he had concluded his remarks, a faculty member stood and asked, "Why do I need religion? I am a good person. I treat others decently. I lead an honest and ethical life. What does religion have to offer me?" Professor Heschel replied, "That is the difference between you and me. You are a good person. I am not." Religion can heighten our awareness of our moral imperfection—not to undermine us, but to give us a target to shoot for.

Religion can also hold the target steady. Religiously mandated obligations resist the often shifting winds of cultural or political correctness. When we are urged by those we respect to embrace a certain approach on Monday, and then presented, from another quarter, with a passionate case for contradictory behavior on Tuesday, what are we to do? How am I to evaluate the relevance of situational factors to judgments about morality? (For instance, when is it permissible to kill or to lie?) Which prohibitions should be discarded as arcane, and which ones should be eternal? How do I hit a moving target? Where do I aim?

I once heard a minister screaming at his congregation: "Temptation is all around us. Only by embracing Jesus will you find the strength to resist." Indeed, there are many religiously faithful who believe that the only reasonable basis for morality is the fear of ultimate punishment. If you know you are not going to get caught, what's to stop you from stealing? they rhetorically ask.

The question is predicated on a view of man as more powerfully driven by evil impulses than by good ones. The Apostle Paul, in the New Testament, declares, "I know that nothing good dwells within me." (Romans 7:18) For centuries, the Church taught that we are all sinners, incapable of overcoming our sinful nature without divine assistance. With the rise of Protestantism in the sixteenth century, the conviction deepened that our nature was completely evil. Martin Luther, for example, believed that "we are utterly depraved."

But man can be moral apart from belief in a transcendent being, if he refuses to accept such a pessimistic view of his nature. Many of us act honestly even when there would be no chance of detecting our dishonesty. Many of us act generously even when there is no public recognition of that deed. There were morals long before there was a philosophy or religion of morality.

Why be moral if there is no God? Secularists would offer many reasons: (1) They would point to the spontaneous caring in very young children as evidence of our true nature. (2) They would argue that living morally and creating a just universe, *in and of themselves*, can provide their past, present, and future with life-affirming meaning. (3) They would insist that morality is simply necessary in order to prevent social chaos and mutual destruction, and that human beings have the capacity to understand their dependence on one another.

In many minds, religion is associated with authority, authority is associated with parental discipline, and parental discipline is associated with the resentment of being forced to bend to another's will. As adults, we feel the pleasure of broken shackles and exclaim: Now I can do whatever I want! We are forevermore wary of any seeming curtailment of our autonomy.

Partly to assuage our suspicion of religion's encroachment on our autonomy, clergymen emphasize that we all have free will. Ultimately, *we* must make the decisions and choices, they remind us. For example, despite the Catholic Church's unwavering approaches to certain life predicaments (such as abortion, contraception, and divorce), Vatican Council II understood our need for independence as well:

Authentic freedom is an exceptional sign of the divine image within man. For God has willed that man be left "in the hand of his own counsel" (Sir. 15:4) so that he can seek his creator spontaneously and come freely to utter and blissful perfection through loyalty to him. Hence, man's dignity demands that he act according to a knowing and free choice. Such a choice is personally motivated and prompted from within. It does not result from blind internal impulse or from mere external pressure.

There will always be those who resist any restraints on their freedom. They will abhor religion because religion demands commitments. For individuals who are predominantly focused on self and freedom, religious morality appears excessive, its practitioners zealots. I recently heard a local clergyman say that if Moses came down from Mount Sinai today, he would have to offer the Ten Suggestions.

Moral precepts clear a path for us to follow. Still, for many of us, life is a riddle, a puzzle, a conundrum. We search for its meaning, for its ambition. The seventeenth-century French scientist and moral philosopher, Pascal, wrote in *Pensées* and the *Provincial Letters*:

> When I consider the short duration of my life, swallowed up in the eternity before and after, the little space which I fill, and even can see, engulfed in the infinite immensity of spaces of which I am ignorant, and which know me not, I am frightened, and am astonished at being here rather than there; for there is no reason why here rather than there, why now rather than then. Who has put me here? By whose order and direction has this place and time been allotted me?

God provides a purpose. He wants us to do good.

A challenge:
If you believe in God, choose one day in the coming week and live it as if God is always looking over your shoulder.
If you do not believe in God, choose one day in the coming week and live it as if God is always looking over your shoulder.

CHAPTER THREE

When We Fail to Be Moral

EMOTIONS CAN GET IN THE WAY OF DOING what's right.

There is a sardonic joke about a wealthy shopkeeper who is on his way home before the Sabbath arrives. Every week, he takes the same route, passes a blind beggar on a corner, and drops a few coins in the unfortunate's tin cup. This afternoon, however, he walks past the beggar without making any offering.

"Sir, you forgot to drop something in my cup," the beggar calls to him.

"I'm sorry. It was a bad week in the business," answers the shopkeeper.

"So, because you had a bad week, I should suffer?"

I am firmly convinced that we would rather be generous, fair, forgiving, and compassionate, than stingy, selfish, begrudging, and insensitive. But we have all suffered deep disappointments, are enslaved by our anger, and driven to distraction by our insecurities. We cheat when we feel weak or to prove our power and invincibility (which is merely a reflection of our sense of deep-seated impotence).

We act insensitively when we harbor the most self-doubt. When we are preoccupied with our self and our perceived shortcomings, we are precluded from accurately perceiving and responding to the needs of others. Conversely, when we are happy and, as a result, not as self-absorbed, we are more generous with our empathy and assistance.

I read a recent article about the richest people in America (no one under three hundred million was listed) and how many of them fail to make *any* charitable contributions. My guess is these are individuals who, despite their wealth, still retain a fundamental sense of deprivation. When I feel deprived, I lose touch with any sentiment of obligation beyond myself. I lose my ability to care about you. And, clearly, it is my *perception* of my portion in life, and not any objective measurement of it, that will determine my behavior. Regardless of my ability to reason morally, to know what's right, if I feel unfulfilled and frustrated, I won't act from my higher, giving self.

So often, when we are unhappy, we have this amorphous feeling in our gut that the world has done us wrong, that life has dealt us a bad hand. When I feel this way, I righteously reject any claim coming from the outside. Not only do I owe others nothing, but I permit myself to act indecently to you because I feel as though life has acted indecently to me.

When we feel deprived, we get angry, but we don't necessarily feel weaker. Anxiety, however, undermines our basic confidence. It obscures our view of our capabilities. As a result, when I am anxious, I believe I must husband all of my attention and effort in order to meet upcoming challenges. There is none of me, therefore, left over to care for you. Unfortunately, this dynamic affects not only you and me, but those who presumably are most attuned to moral issues.

A camouflaged psychological experiment provided dramatic illustration of how situational pressures can sometimes overwhelm the highest moral principle. Seminarians at the Princeton Theological

Seminary were asked to prepare a short presentation on the parable of the Good Samaritan as described in the New Testament:

> A man was going down from Jerusalem to Jericho, and he fell among robbers, who stripped him and beat him and departed, leaving him half dead. Now by chance a priest was going down the road; and when he saw him he passed by on the other side. So likewise a Levite, when he came to the place and saw him, passed by on the other side. But a Samaritan, as he journeyed, came to where he was; and when he saw him, he had compassion, and went to him and bound his wounds, pouring on oil and wine; then he set him on his own beast and brought him to an inn, and took care of him. And the next day he took out two dennarii and gave them to the innkeeper, saying, "Take care of him; and whatever more you spend, I will repay you when I come back." Which of these three, do you think, proved neighbor to him who fell among the robbers? He said, "The one who showed mercy on him." And Jesus said, . . . "Go and do likewise." (Luke 10:29–37)

The seminarians were then asked to deliver their presentation in a building across the campus from where they received their instructions. The researchers manipulated how rushed the subjects felt (that is, how anxious). In the "high-hurry" condition, the students were told, "Oh, you're late. They were expecting you a few minutes ago. You'd better get moving." In the "intermediate-hurry" condition, the students were told, "The assistant is ready for you, so please go over." In the "low-hurry" condition, the students were informed, "It'll be a few minutes before they're ready for you, but you might as well head over."

Along the seminarians' path, the experimenter's confederate was slumped over, shabbily dressed, coughing, and groaning. He clearly needed help. Whether or not the seminarian stopped to assist the man in seeming need depended most on the time factor. Subjects who were under great time pressure (that is, anxious) were much less likely to stop and help than those not so pressed. The authors of the study, John Darley and C. Daniel Batson, wrote: "Indeed, on several occasions, a seminary student going to give his talk on the parable of the Good Samaritan literally stepped over the victim as he hurried on his way."

It would be easy to view these seminarians as hypocrites who did not practice what they preached. But this interpretation would be too simplistic. Some of the hurried students scarcely looked at the victim because they were so focused on their task at hand. But those who were struck by the plight of the victim found themselves in a conflict. Do I fulfill my responsibility to the experimenter, or do I help the sick stranger? Darley and Batson noted, "Conflict, rather than callousness, can explain their failure to stop." Nevertheless, when we feel pressed, we tend to lose sight of moral priorities.

How many of us, on so many occasions, have noticed someone in emotional or physical need and simply rushed by because we felt so pressured by our own concerns? How many of us have been face-to-face with another's quivering lip or teary eyes and decided to sidestep the issue with the thought: "I don't want to open that can of worms and then have to deal with it."

There Are No Moral People

WE OFTEN REFER TO A PERSON'S "MORAL CHARACTER." THE USE OF the word *character* implies a consistency, a point of view that will be activated no matter what the circumstance. But we are not nearly as steadfast as we might at first believe. People do not live out generalized codes of moral behavior. There are no moral people. Instead, our readiness to behave morally will be influenced by:

(1) the reward/cost/risk ratio—the potential reward (psychological and/or physical and/or material) of our immoral behavior

balanced against the potential cost (punishment) of our behavior should it be uncovered, and an assessment of the likelihood of either;

(2) how we might justify or rationalize our behavior in this
particular situation;

(3) how capable we are of resisting temptation at any particular
moment; that is, how deprived we feel;

(4) the external pressures we are under (for example, if I have
a sick child and need money to pay for medicine, I will be
more likely to steal if I don't have it);

(5) which moral issues are most salient to us (for example, not
lying to my wife may be on my moral agenda, but kindness
to strangers may not be).

Actually, we are quite adept at moral flexibility. I know of a news-
paper columnist whose views on public policy (such as affirmative
action, welfare reform, educational vouchers) and private behavior
(such as abortion and divorce) are conservative all down the line,
except for one area—sexuality. When it comes to public pornogra-
phy, clubs with naked dancers, or private sexual practices like pre-
marital sex or adultery, moral rules, for this columnist, are no longer
inviolate. (I have heard him say, "You have to ask, 'Why did he
commit adultery?' Perhaps he and his wife were emotionally estranged from one another. Perhaps he was feeling rejected.") It happens that this columnist had, himself, lived a life where he felt free
to express his sexuality in a rather casual, liberal manner. (I can't
help but wonder how he would react if he were the victim of his
wife's infidelity.) We find all sorts of convoluted means to maintain
not only a self-image of goodness, but one that possesses high moral
standards, as well. While we try to behave in ways that are consistent
with our moral principles, *we amend those principles to justify our
behavior.*

Earlier you saw how feelings of deprivation can affect our desire to care for others. We will also withdraw into a self-protective shell when we perceive the world not to care for us. As you read in Chapter One, a child requires a supportive, nurturing, consistent adult in order to establish a basic trust in humanity. Without that early experience, his impulse to fairness and justice will recede.

I tune out your concerns when I feel that no one cares about me. And I get even angrier when I feel directly abused. There is a clear link between our inclination to cruelty and our having been treated with cruelty as a child. When fathers humiliate their sons, a rage is born. That rage, unfortunately, spreads far beyond its initial target. For an abused child who grows to adulthood, the entire world becomes a dangerous and unfair antagonist. In his most helpless moments, times when he feels as though he has so little control over his life, this damaged soul will play out the script he has been dealt: Having felt so powerless before, he thinks, "I will do everything I can not to be vulnerable again. I will attack you before you attack me."

Philosophers and theologians have long debated our essential nature. Are we good or evil? But we are not static vessels. We are not good *or* evil. Our hurt, frightened self engages in a continuous tug-of-war with our higher, moral self. Those who feel they have been cheated in life are often determined that others must be cheated as well. After all, what's fair? One of our tasks is to help others feel safe enough, secure enough, and cared about enough, so they can choose kindness over callousness.

How Justifications Help Us Act Immorally

AS WE SAW WITH THE CONSERVATIVE COLUMNIST, OUR MORAL JUDGment is tossed about by our needs and desires. We find ways to rationalize issues that are most personally difficult. So, too, our moral outrage picks and chooses its targets. We decide which subjects warrant our focus and define our sense of moral rectitude accordingly.

However, we often deny our impulse to *act* morally by denying any personal responsibility to alleviate the suffering at hand. Our conscience is assuaged by our vague sense that others will provide assistance because the need is so apparent. If necessary to justify our inaction, we may go further and deny any urgency or deservedness in the first place.

We all know there are children who go to bed hungry, impoverished, and diseased. Yet we allow this suffering to continue while we pursue comparatively frivolous (and often expensive) goals. To an outside observer, we would seem indifferent, even cynical, about the misery of others. But to ourselves, we must maintain a self-perception of benevolence.

So we cling to a belief in what psychologists call "the Just World Hypothesis." In order to make sense of the environment and avoid the anxiety-producing perception that the world operates on a random basis, we believe that people get what they deserve. I want to believe that bad things happen to bad people and that, because I am basically a good person, misfortune will not befall me as it does to those less deserving. When we read about the rape of a woman in a parking lot, we think, "She shouldn't have walked to her car alone at night."

When someone else is hurt, it threatens us. We therefore believe that the hurt individual is a faulty person and deserves his misfortune. When anyone runs into difficulties because of his own irresponsibility or recklessness, it's up to the person to bail himself out. "You've made your bed, now lie in it," we say. And because, as I just mentioned, we tend to believe that people get what they deserve, that phrase provides a double dose of justification for withholding help or sympathy to someone who we say is unworthy of it in the first place.

We are particularly egregious in our misplaced attributions when we personally harm another and have no concern about making amends. It is in those situations that we dismiss any consideration of our own malevolence and simply blame the victim: "Serves him right for being so naive!" For some, merely observing an innocent victim wronged is sufficient excuse to derogate him. I recently saw a gang member interviewed on a documentary. He explained why he beat in a teenage boy's head with a lead pipe until the sixteen-year-old was unconscious: "He had no business bein' in my neighborhood. The dumb fuckhead shoulda known better. If he wasn't where he wasn't supposed to be, I wouldn'ta had to do it to him."

"Are you sure the boy knew he wasn't supposed to be on that street?" the interviewer asked.

A second gang member, who was there when the boy was beaten, laughed. "If he didn't, he sure was a dumb mother."

People who commit evil deeds are often more deficient in compassion and empathy than in their ability to reason morally. The highest concepts of justice, the common welfare, the good of the people, God, and freedom have been used to justify atrocities. The philosopher Pascal observed, "Evil is never done so thoroughly or so well as when it is done with a good conscience."

Because we need to believe we are good, we only note the *intention* behind our deeds, and not their consequences. The devout Nazis who slaughtered millions of innocent civilians only *intended* to be good soldiers, loyal Germans. A more personal example: When my son, Nathan, was born, there were serious complications that placed him in the intensive care unit after delivery. When we finally brought him home, he was still somewhat fragile. It was the middle of winter, and when I attempted to turn on the heat, it would not ignite. I called the gas company.

"Could you please send someone out to my home. My heater won't work and I have a sick infant whom I just brought back from the hospital."

"I'm sorry, sir. We can't have anyone out there for forty-eight hours after we receive a request."

"But you don't understand. I have a sick infant. It's very cold in my house, and I'm afraid it might place him in real danger."

"I'm sorry, sir. That's the policy. If there is no gas leak, the earliest I can have someone out is forty-eight hours."

"But this is an unusual situation. I can't wait forty-eight hours."

"I'm only telling you what the rules are, sir."

The woman on the other end of the line was only trying to do her job well. Her job was to adhere strictly to the policies of her company and not allow unspecified exceptions. In fact, she was doing her job well, as it was defined by her superiors. She put me off despite my assertive pleas. More important, she felt good about herself because she had accomplished what she was paid to do. She had not been asked to consider the consequences of her actions or the policy that drove them.

Bill Nash, husband and father of two teenage boys, was successful, rich, and feeling his age. His wife of twenty-two years had recently discovered that he was having an affair. In a plaintive tone of voice, Bill told me how he looked at it: "You know, I wasn't *trying* to hurt her. Believe me. She wasn't supposed to find out! It was something I did for me. I just needed a boost. . . . I have it all . . . but I feel empty. There's no joy in my life. I'm forty-eight, with a paunch, and losing my hair. . . . I wanted to feel special to someone . . . that someone would find me exciting. . . . I love my wife. I never had any intention of going anywhere. . . . This had nothing to do with our marriage. Marlene should understand that. I guess you could call it a midlife crisis. It shouldn't be such a big deal."

The absence of any guilt on Bill's part reflected his exclusive focus on his intentions. Bill Nash didn't want to hurt anyone. Bill just wanted to feel "special" again. The Nazi murderers, the gas company employee, and Bill Nash all displayed a failure to understand a core, moral issue: While we may *feel* responsible only for what we intend, we *are* responsible for all that we do.

Immoral Contagion

THE BALANCE BETWEEN OUR SELFISH IMPULSES AND OUR CONSIDER-
ate ones, between our fears and our goodness, is a delicate one. The
scales are easily tipped in either direction. It's comforting, therefore,
to be surrounded by compassionate people. They encourage us by
their mere example. By shining a light on the path of justice, they
help dispel our misgivings and move us forward with them.

You are out shopping and pass someone collecting money to help
the homeless, provide food for the hungry, or clothe the poor. Do
you reach into your pocket or purse to make a contribution?

You are more likely to if you observe someone else do it. The
mere presence of coins or bills in the collection box acts as an
encouragement. In an analogous experimental setup, a young
woman stood next to a Ford Mustang with a flat tire in a residential
area of Los Angeles. Passing motorists who had seen a man from a
different car (and presumably a stranger) helping another woman
change a tire a quarter of a mile back were almost twice as likely
to stop and help as motorists who had not previously observed that
kind of assistance.

Helpful, generous people inspire. They are reminders of the
choices we have before us. They invite our compassionate, tender
self to emerge and breathe.

But we are also highly susceptible to the reverse process. Seeing
others act immorally activates our readily available justifications for
doing likewise. When we see others act cruelly, our own primitive
impulses seek an opening. When the malevolence is *group*-inspired,
we feel even more emboldened, as our concerns about retaliation are
relieved. We feel more powerful when our energies are harnessed to
an already moving train. We feel more invincible and correct when
we are surrounded by others who are animated by the same objec-
tives. When rioters in Los Angeles were asked why they were looting,
many replied, "Everybody's doing it!" If everyone's doing it, how

can it be wrong? And if everyone's doing it, I won't be singled out and punished, because I can lose myself in the crowd.

Being a part of a group may have other consequences that inhibit a sense of accountability as well. When we act in concert with others, our self-awareness is fogged, and we lose touch with our internal standards. When we act in concert with others, a sense of anonymity overcomes us. Now, no one is responsible because this is a group undertaking.

Anonymity can unshackle our aggressive impulses even when we act alone. The military keenly understands the importance of developing a sense of anonymity in their recruits in order to unleash their combative nature. Under conditions of high emotional arousal (a screaming drill sergeant), designed to have the individual lose touch with any internal compass, we shave the recruit's head and provide him with the same uniform as the hundreds of young men who surround him. In other words, we strip him of his individuality and identity.

At first glance, one's intelligence and one's ability to reason morally seem highly correlated. But the follow-through is another matter. History is replete with instances of highly intelligent people who acted in a corrupt fashion. In fact, the relationship between intelligence and honesty often declines when one's risk of getting caught is low. (It takes brains to devise shell companies and employ offshore banks to shelter one's ill-gotten gains.) The brake of our intelligence loses its traction when no one is watching. Furthermore, this decline is hastened when we view others acting dishonestly. My *fear* kicks in when I observe you cheating because I now perceive myself to be at a disadvantage. There is also my pride. When I perceive everyone around me "stretching the limits" of the tax code, I feel like a sucker for strictly abiding by the rules.

Being able to act morally in the face of others who do not is particularly difficult for adolescents. Teenagers are highly sensitive to the approbation of their peers; they are dying for acceptance. Their sense of who they are and what they stand for is also in flux.

But this exaggerated need for approval and acceptance lingers for many of us into adulthood. After all, from our earliest days, we learn that agreeing with others close by, and behaving much as they do, causes them to like us. And because we most want to be accepted by friends and those we admire, we are also readily influenced by their attitudes and actions.

We may not ape another's immoral behavior, but we also do not stand up and say to a friend, a colleague, or even a neighbor, "I think that what you did is wrong." Evidence for how difficult this can be is provided by your responses to the following two questions: (1) How many times, after viewing someone act in an unjust or inconsiderate manner, have you thought to yourself, "That's wrong"? (2) How many times have you said that to the offending individual? If you are like most of us, the answer to the first question is probably, "Hundreds." The answer to the second question reflects our failure of courage.

Teenagers will often go along with immoral behavior because they not only want to seem "cool," but also because they want to demonstrate their loyalty to the group. "Good Germans" did the same. They wanted to prove that they were committed to the German nation, the German people, and their shared destiny. Most of us average individuals simply want "to get along," to fit in. We are terrified of anyone saying, "What's wrong with him?"

Everyone's Values Do Not Have Equal Merit

WE HAVE BEEN TOLD THAT THE ANSWER TO THE QUESTION, "WHAT is right?" is completely subjective, up to each individual to decide for himself. We have been reassured that everyone's values have equal merit. Addressing midlife, Gail Sheehy writes in her book *Passages:*

> Let go. Let it happen to you. Let it happen to your partner. Let the feelings. Let the changes.

You can't take everything with you when you leave on the midlife journey. You are moving away. Away from institutional claims and other people's agenda. Away from external valuations and accreditations, in search of an inner validation. You are moving out of roles and into the self. If I could give everyone a gift for the send-off on this journey, it would be a tent. A tent for tentativeness. The gift of portable roots.

To reach the clearing beyond, we must stay with the weightless journey through uncertainty. Whatever the counterfeit safety we hold from overinvestments in people and institutions must be given up. The inner custodian must be unseated from the controls. No foreign power can direct our journey from now on. It is for each of us to find a course that is valid by our own reckoning.

By only emphasizing the uniqueness of each of us, Sheehy forgets our commonality. By focusing on the primacy of autonomy, she undercuts values that breed continuity and enhance relationship. By permitting us only to attend to the self, she excuses an absence of compassion. By encouraging judgment in isolation, she forgets *common* courtesy.

We cannot allow each person to choose for himself what is moral. He will inevitably be swayed by his emotions and individual needs. He will opt for convenience. We must all accept a minimum, basic morality. A morality, for example, that respects the rights of others and encourages compassion for the troubled is superior to one that places the self at the center of one's attention.

It's Every Man for Himself

WE ARE BOMBARDED WITH STRATEGIES FOR *INDIVIDUAL* FULFILLMENT: how to win, how to succeed, how to lure a mate, how to express your anger, how to stand up for yourself. All of these strategies are important, but the singular emphasis on the self is ultimately isolating and immoral. None of these paths to happiness include a discussion of our obligations to others.

In their important book, *Habits of the Heart*, Robert Bellah, Richard Madsen, William Sullivan, Ann Swidler, and Steven Tipton contrast the effects of an individual versus a more communal orientation. One of those they interviewed was Margaret Oldham, a highly successful psychotherapist in her early thirties:

In Margaret's view, the most important thing in life is doing whatever you choose to do as well as you can. Summing up her sense of the meaning of life, she says: "I just sort of accept the way the world is and then don't think about it a whole lot. I tend to operate on the assumption that what I want to do and what I feel like is what I should do. What I think the universe wants from me is to take my values, *whatever they might happen to be* [my emphasis], and live up to them as much as I can. If I'm the best person I know how to be according to my lights, then something good will happen. I think in a lot of ways living that kind of life is its own reward in and of itself.

For Margaret Oldham and many others, decisions about personal behavior must be made autonomously and must solely emanate from an internal guiding source. Freedom implies being unencumbered by the demands of anyone else. Freedom, for many, implies freedom from any constraints of consideration. Bellah and his colleagues write:

Freedom is perhaps the most resonant, deeply held American value. In some ways, it defines the good in both personal and political life. Yet freedom turns out to mean being left alone by others, not having other people's values, ideas, or styles of life forced upon one, being free of arbitrary authority in work, family, and political life. What it is that one might do with that freedom is much more difficult for Americans to define. And if the entire social world is made up of individuals, each endowed with the right to be free of others' demands, it becomes hard to forge bonds of attachment to, or cooperation with, other people, since such bonds would imply obligations that necessarily impinge on one's freedom. Thus, Margaret Oldham, for example, sets great store on becoming an autonomous person, responsible for her own life, and she recognizes that other people, like herself, are free to have their own values and to lead their lives the way they choose. But then, by the same token, if she doesn't like what they do or the way they live, her only right is the right to walk away. In some sense, for her, freedom to be left alone is a freedom that implies being alone.

Don't bother me and I won't bother you.

The emphasis on self-reliance as a virtue implies a disconnectedness from others. Oftentimes, this virtue springs from a certain cynicism and deep mistrust of others. Jesse Franklin, a forty-six-year-old talent agent, doesn't have any friends. As he told me during one of our sessions: "Eventually the person, your 'friend,' is going to disappoint you because, basically, people are selfish. When it comes right down to it, you can't really rely on anyone because it's every man for himself."

"In the end, you're alone," is the commonly accepted existential wisdom. But it is not true. In the end, I am in this with you because your actions affect me and my actions affect you. Because Jesse Franklin believes that he can't expect anything from anyone, that belief also limits the demands he feels he can make on anyone. Jesse Franklin doesn't ask for any consideration. Nevertheless, he angrily trudges through life resenting my assumed indifference to him.

When a couple is being counseled, it is commonplace for the therapist to have the individuals explicitly state what they want from each other. What is often missing, however, is an acknowledgment of what would be best for the *relationship*. When we solely focus on individual emotional gratification as the criteria for remaining in a relationship, we lose sight of the value of the commitments we have made and must make.

I remember a former teacher, Dr. Walter Brackelmanns, telling us about one therapy session he had with a very angry, unhappy couple. As usual in this circumstance, each individual presented his or her case and was firmly convinced that "Not only am I right, but if you could only do what I ask we could have a much better relationship." At one point, when the husband was not receiving the hoped-for affirmation of the correctness of his position, he turned to Dr. Brackelmanns and asked, "Whose side are you on, anyway?" To which Dr. Brackelmanns replied, "I'm on the side of the marriage."

I am one of those who are appalled at the casualness with which some people approach divorce, particularly when children are in the picture. After hearing that our parents' and grandparents' generations accepted a frustration-filled, unsatisfying life because they stayed together "for the sake of the children," we have reacted with the bromide: Better to divorce than have a child grow up in a tension-filled environment. "Children are very resilient, they'll be okay," we are reassured. But any family that has experienced divorce knows that the children are never simply "okay." Children of divorce are hurt, angry, confused, guilty, and frightened. For some, the wounds of mistrust and helplessness take many years and not a few relationships to heal over. One should not remain in an acrimonious, destructive, irreparable marriage for the sake of the children. But let's not kid ourselves about the serious consequences of that decision.

Paula, a forty-one-year-old attorney, and Daniel, a forty-two-year-old screenwriter, had been married for sixteen years. They had a thirteen-year-old daughter, Diana, and a twelve-year-old son, Isaac. Both Paula and Daniel had been terribly unhappy with each other for several years. Recently, Daniel had felt so hopeless that he was aware of suicidal thoughts. Paula and Daniel's complaints were common ones: You're selfish, you don't really listen to me, you're not supportive of what I do, you said things to me that I can never forget and never forgive. Both Paula and Daniel had decided that the marriage was over for them, but they would not divorce because they didn't want to damage their children. They would wait to separate until Diana and Isaac were older and away in college.

What they wanted to discuss with me was how they could maintain a marriage while living essentially disconnected lives. My response was, "Your commitment to your children is admirable. But if your only commitment is to your children, then you will be more depressed and angry in six or seven years than you are now. If you are going to remain together, let's work on making this marriage a better one." We fulfill ourselves not apart from one another, but through our relationship to one another. Three months into therapy, Paula and Daniel were able to reconnect, move past their anger, and rediscover their mutual love. They had weathered another one of those seemingly inescapable downturns in a lifetime partnership.

When I Know What I Should Do, But Don't

EVERY DAY, I DON'T DO WHAT I KNOW I SHOULD:

 I should have called my friend to see how his father's surgery went.
 I should have sat down with my child to ask about the math test she took today instead of fleetingly calling to her from the next room, "How did your test go, sweetie?"
 I should have been more patient with my wife this morning

when she tried to explain what was wrong with our water heater.

I should have found out why my seventy-seven-year-old mother didn't call me yesterday like she said she would.

I should have written a bigger check for that charity.

Obviously I, like most people, display a serious gap between what I say and what I do. Sometimes, I behave insensitively because I feel the pressure of whatever task is at hand. At other times, I don't behave as I should because I feel overwhelmed and barely able to juggle all the necessary balls in the air at the same time. Frequently, I just feel hurried. No wonder studies consistently demonstrate that individuals living in rural areas are more helpful than urban dwellers. Those living in the countryside slow life down and allow room to care. They are also spared the daily onslaught of city stimuli that distract us from focusing on what's really important. In the city, I observe people rushing. Do they know something I don't know? I worry. Will they get there before I do?

Besides the internal anxieties and external distractions that keep us from being more sensitive to the needs of others, we have also been socialized in a culture that emphasizes individualism and does not consider helping to be a moral imperative. Psychologists Joan Miller, David Bersoff, and Robin Harwood of Yale University presented American and Indian subjects with stories about people who refused to give help to another person. The need for help varied. In some stories, the need was extreme (the person needed mouth-to-mouth resuscitation) and in others it wasn't (the person needed directions to a store). In addition, the relationship between the person needing help and the person refusing to give help varied. In some stories, people refused help to their young children, in others their best friends, and in others, strangers. After reading the stories, subjects were asked whether the person who refused to give help was morally obliged to provide assistance.

The results showed that the Americans' judgments of moral obligation were much more influenced than Indians' by the degree of need and by the nature of the relationship between helper and beneficiary. Specifically, the Americans believed that people are morally obligated to help when the situation is life-threatening and when they are closely related to the person needing help. In contrast, the Indians believed that people are more universally obligated to help. Unless there are compelling needs and close personal relationships that warrant helping, Americans tend to believe that individuals are free to "do their own thing." Indians, on the other hand, view helping as an obligation woven into the social fabric.

One of the reasons for the discrepancy between our ability to reason morally (which is often quite high) and our willingness to behave morally (which often leaves something to be desired) is that the intellectual exercise of figuring out "What's the right thing to do in this dilemma?" takes place during "cool time," a time of unhurriedness conducive to reflection. Moral emergencies, on the other hand, take place during "hot time," a time of real-life pressures, competing impulses, emotional arousal, and confusion.

Take the infamous case of Kitty Genovese. On March 13, 1964, at 3:20 A.M., Kitty Genovese was returning home from her job as manager of a bar. She had parked her car and was about to enter her apartment building. Suddenly a man ran up to her brandishing a knife. She ran, but he chased her, caught up, and stabbed her repeatedly. Kitty screamed for help, and lights came on in many of the apartment windows that overlooked the scene. The attacker started to leave, but for some reason he returned and resumed his assault on the screaming Kitty. In total, the attack lasted forty-five minutes, and when it was over, Kitty Genovese lay dead. Afterward, thirty-eight people reported that they had heard her scream, but not a single individual offered assistance or even placed a call to the police.

Why not? Many commentators suggested that the bystanders were unresponsive because our society had become apathetic, selfish, and indifferent to the plight of others. While the explanation satisfies our moral outrage, it may not be true. Social psychologists John Darley and Bibb Latane, discussing the Genovese story over lunch, proposed a different explanation for why people failed to help. (They later found support for their theory in many experimental situations.) When we are in a group and confronted by an emergency, we experience a diffusion of personal responsibility. It is as if each person in the group says to himself or herself, "Maybe somebody else will do it."

There are countless ways to avoid our responsibility to come to the aid of another. We may not notice (or pretend not to notice) the plight, may notice it but decide that it is the fault of the victim, or may believe that someone else is better equipped to handle it. When other bystanders are present, it is easier to pretend not to notice, easier to allow others to decide if the victim deserves help, and easier to avoid a sense of personal responsibility.

Oftentimes, there is some degree of ambiguity in emergency situations, so potential helpers hold back and wait for additional "information" in order to be sure what is going on. The more ambiguous the situation, the less likely people are to offer assistance. For example, if we see a man and woman fighting, we are more likely to intervene if we are certain they are strangers than if they are married ("It's only a lovers' quarrel"). If, however, the nature of their relationship is not apparent, we hesitate. Finally, because it is easier *not* to help than to actively intervene, we are especially attentive to any cues that suggest there is no reason to be concerned. Therefore, multiple bystanders can, by their passivity, inadvertently communicate to one another that everything is as it should be.

Leaving my office late one night, I passed a woman sobbing in the long corridor leading to the elevator. Should I say something? I continued walking, feeling a little remiss, but noticing that she was leaning against the door of another psychologist, I assumed that she had just emerged from a session and was feeling its aftereffects. Not a big deal, it happens all the time, I thought. However, as I waited for the elevator to arrive, I became increasingly uneasy. What if my assumption was wrong? What if she hadn't just ended a psychotherapy session? And, even if she had, why shouldn't I offer help? I went back. "Are you all right?" I asked. "Yes," she replied. "I just got out of a painful therapy hour. I'll be okay." My original assumption about the cause of her tears had been correct. But so what? I still had a duty to inquire, to make that gesture.

Either alone or in the midst of a group, we have all been in a situation where we spotted someone in need. As you can see, there are many potential inhibitors we must overcome before we extend ourselves. In addition to those factors already mentioned, we may not know how to help or what to do. Nevertheless, there are two approaches you can always employ: (1) Express your concern to the victim, and (2) Ask the victim if he or she would like your assistance. Reach out. Don't ignore.

Bridging the Gap

WE MAY HAVE MORAL CONVICTIONS. WE MAY HAVE MATURE MORAL judgment. But neither of these necessarily lead us to moral *behavior*. Bridging the gap between our beliefs and our actions requires a resoluteness, a commitment, not a feeling.

Feelings are fickle. Obligation, on the other hand, produces consistency and staying power. Morality doesn't always "pay," at least in the short run. We must be moved, therefore, by a loftier motive than self-interest, one with a longer perspective than the present moment. While feelings quickly evaporate, a sense of duty lasts.

Many people have chosen to dichotomize acting out of obligation and acting out of love. The latter is often proposed as the healthier of the two motives. In fact, we often recoil from the entire notion of obligation: "Why should I do it if I don't feel like it? Wouldn't that be hypocritical? I've got to be true to myself!" Indeed, it would not be hypocritical to do what's right, even if you do not feel like it. On the contrary, having a sense of obligation beyond oneself is one of the premier indicators of moral health.

Aristotle understood how easily our actions are swayed by momentary passions and derailed from a just track. While moral qualities are natural attributes within each of us, we nevertheless need to develop disciplined habits, he wrote. It is by practicing justice that we develop a just character. And if, at first, our feelings lag behind, the repetition of our actions will bring them up to speed. We all might prefer our behavior to spring from our feelings. But behavior can *stimulate* feelings as well. George Eliot, the nineteenth-century English novelist, wrote, "Our deeds determine us, as much as we determine our deeds."

Forty-eight-year-old Andy Bostwick was a very rich clothing manufacturer and a very stingy person. As is the case with many people who hoard their money, Andy was driven by fantasies of poverty and homelessness. But Andy wanted to get into an exclusive country club. The country club required that a prospective member show evidence of a minimum of fifty thousand dollars in annual charitable contributions. So, beginning two years prior to his application for membership, Andy breathed deeply and wrote the checks. Today, Andy is fifty-eight and has been enormously enjoying the golfing camaraderie at the club over the past decade. He has also increased his gifts to the needy each and every one of the past ten years, to a point where he is being honored at the club as its Man of the Year. He recently confided, "You know it's done me good to be more charitable. I feel better about myself. I'm more relaxed now. I always made a lot of money. But so what? What did I have at the end of the day? Just more money. Now, I feel like I always want to do more."

We must also be aware of our excuses. You have probably heard some variation of the line, "Real life doesn't lend itself to hard and fast rules." Abhorring the notion of fixed obligations, some individuals have already taken one step down the road of self-justification. Before we make any public apologies for our inconsiderate behavior, we must first be able to acknowledge to ourself: "I was wrong." We must be able to give up some of our self-righteousness.

Don't expect too little of yourself, but don't expect too much, either. People don't change overnight. However, when we do change for the better, when we take small steps toward greater generosity, increased considerateness, and respect for the dignity of others, we feel disproportionately elevated. It feels good to do good.

When we throw our hands up in the air and say, "I can't do anything about all the starving children in the world," we paralyze ourselves. Of course you can't do anything about *all* the starving children in the world, but you can do something about *one*. We are taught that "Whoever saves one life, saves the world entire."

Closer to home, you can do something thoughtful and unexpected for a loved one, an acquaintance, or a stranger. Long ago, psychologists discovered the key to moving forward and tackling a big job — break the task into small "bits," segments that are readily doable, and then keep going to the next "bit." Changing lifelong patterns is a big job. But as your accomplishments mount, your confidence will grow and your fears will wane.

It would be great if you acted more considerately and sensitively out of love and generosity. But if those impulses are not apparent, the next best alternative is acting justly because you should. What we think about while acting can be helpful. Instead of the "cost" (material or psychological) of the gesture, focus on the good that will come of it. And remember that there is a part of you that wants to do what's right.

A suggested visualization: Imagine that you are made up of two pots of soil. Growing in one pot is your generous, considerate, compassionate life force. Growing in the other pot is your insecure, angry, selfish spirit. Water the first pot, even once a week. Allow the soil of the second pot to dry up and die.

Baby Ruths and Nonpareils

WHEN I WAS A KID, I OCCASIONALLY STOLE A BABY RUTH BAR OR A box of Nonpareils from the candy store on the corner of Nostrand Avenue and Avenue K in Brooklyn. As I left the store without hearing, "Hey, kid, what do you think you're doing?!" I breathed a sigh of relief and assumed, "No harm, no foul." No big deal (except perhaps the exaltation of having gotten away with something). But there *were* consequences. Today, almost every place of business is equipped with conspicuous video cameras designed to deter widespread theft. My wife was recently stunned by a sign prominently hung in the women's dressing room of a large department store: "This dressing room does not provide complete privacy. Your activities may be monitored by store personnel." Even while we are standing in our underwear, they are going to watch us.

Instead of God looking over our shoulders, we have security monitors. They are continual reminders of the dishonesty lurking in others, and that reminder frightens us. Frightened people are not open, giving people.

I also remember an incident that occurred when I was buying my first home. The seller pointed out a defect that neither I nor my inspector had noticed. While it would cost several hundred dollars to repair, I was overwhelmed with relief. For a moment, at least, I could let go of my suspiciousness and mistrust. A little of *my* goodness was restored.

Our genes carry the propensities for both compassion and heartlessness. Perhaps the best way to tip the scales in favor of virtue is to *promote goodness.* We can do that by our own example. Your kindness will reduce my fears. Your fairness will dampen my wariness. Your generosity will feed my courage.

Close your eyes and imagine this: You and ten thousand others are standing behind a line that has been drawn in the sand. Those who choose to cross the line to the other side commit themselves to fairness, kindness, sensitivity, and compassion. No one is moving. All are held back by the terror of vulnerability. If you step over the line, perhaps thousands of others will follow you. But they need your inspiration. Will you find the courage to lead them?

Some questions for you to ponder:
How do my fears prevent me from acting more fairly?
How do my insecurities prevent me from acting generously?
How does my anger inhibit my compassion?

CHAPTER FOUR

Fairness

THE IDEA IS REALLY RATHER SIMPLE: DO NOT DO to others what you would not want done to you. Yes, the idea is rather simple, but it provides the quintessential moral principle of human relationships.

Somtimes morality appears terribly complex because of competing loyalties, opposing claims, and a myriad of situational variables. But in our day-to-day contacts with loved ones, as well as those more distant, the admonition provides a powerful guiding light: Do not do to others what you would not want done to you.

We find the Golden Rule first articulated in the Book of Leviticus, chapter 19, verse 18, "Love your fellow as yourself, for I am the Eternal One." Hillel, the great teacher living in the first century B.C.E., then employed a slightly different perspective, "What is hateful to you do not do to your neighbor." And in the Book of Matthew (19:16–19), Jesus is asked, "Rabbi, what good thing must I do to receive eternal life?" Jesus replied, "Why do you ask? . . . If you want to enter life, keep the commandments . . . and love your neighbor as yourself."

Seventeen hundred years later, the German philosopher Immanuel Kant paraphrased the Golden Rule and called it the Categorical Imperative. For Kant, each person should be his own moral legislator. But any law we make for ourselves must be one that we would agree to be adopted by all. ("Act as if the maxim of your action by your will were to become a universal law of nature.") For example, if I were to consider breaking a promise, I must weigh whether I would wish all people to have the luxury of breaking their promises.

Philosophers have evolved a variation of the notion of fairness in the principle of reversibility. If I make a decision or propose an agreement that affects you, could I trade places with you and feel good about that decision? Let's say I loan you money at a particular interest rate. If the loan were offered to me, would I feel that the terms of the loan were fair? Or what if I offered to pay for a new fence separating our properties, if you trimmed back the trees overlooking our mutual property line. Would I feel good about the arrangement if I were the one to pay for the trimming, while you took care of the new fence?

The principle of reversibility should not be confined to formal contracts. If I put myself in the shoes of those with whom I interact on even mundane matters, would I be pleased with the way I was being treated? If I were the person waiting on my table in the restaurant, would I feel good about how I was being treated by the customer (that is, me?). If I were one of my students, would I feel that I was being fairly evaluated?

It's a simple way to check yourself. Would you feel good about the way you were dealt with, if you were on the receiving end of your behavior?

"Do unto others as you would have them do unto you" implicitly affirms that we have equal worth simply because we are of one human group. Our impulse to fairness is activated when we recognize that we all have the same essential needs, especially the need to be treated with respect and consideration.

The Balance of Fairness

IN SOUTH AFRICA, THE TRUTH AND RECONCILIATION COMMISSION was recently created in an attempt to heal a nation bloodied and battered by years of racial hatred and political strife. In the final turbulent decade of white rule in South Africa, thousands of people were killed in spasms of violence. The Commission was authorized by the present South African government to investigate the abuses of the previous administrations, particularly its police and military arms. In the interest of cooling racial tensions and staving off a potential military upheaval, the postapartheid Constitution offered immunity from prosecution or civil lawsuits to those who confessed their deeds, no matter how heinous they might have been. The applicants were required to take responsibility for crimes with a political motive between March 1960, when black protestors were massacred by white police at Sharpeville, and May 10, 1994, when Nelson Mandela was inaugurated as the first postapartheid president.

Black South Africans wanted at least an acknowledgment of the vicious persecution they had suffered. Bishop Desmond Tutu is Chairman of the Truth Commission. In an interview conducted by an American journalist in 1996, he was asked if he believed that he and the others on the Commission were honoring the promise of justice they had made to the victims of the repressive regimes. "There are different kinds of justice," he said. "Retributive justice is largely Western. The African understanding is far more restorative—not so much to punish as to redress or restore a balance that has been knocked askew. The justice we hope for is restorative of the dignity of the people." Bishop Tutu wants to assert that black dignity is just as inalienable as white dignity.

We crave dignity and we crave a fairness that produces it. James Wilson, in the *Moral Sense*, describes a game developed by three German economists that illustrates our natural resistance to being treated in a contrary fashion:

Called Ultimatum, it involves two players. The first is given a sum of money—say, ten dollars—that he is to divide in any way he wishes between himself and the second player. The second player must accept or reject the offer, knowing that there will be no further offers, and that the two people will never play the game again. If the second player accepts, the two players divide the money in the way the first player proposed. If the second player rejects the offer, then neither player gets anything. If both players are wholly self-interested, then the first will offer the second one cent and keep $9.99 for himself, and the second player will accept the offer. After all, the second player has no choice: He either gets something or nothing, and one cent is better than nothing. The first player has no incentive to offer more than one cent, since anything more comes out of his share.

If your experience in playing Ultimatum is like that of the German economists who experimented with it, it is extremely unlikely that you will act in a rationally self-interested way. If you are the first player, you will probably propose an equal division of the money or, at worst, something like 70–30. If you are the second player, you will probably reject offers that lopsidedly favor the first player, even though it means you will get nothing. People are willing to forgo money in order to ensure fairness or to punish people who act unfairly—here, the "greedy" first player.

We revolt against unfairness. Several studies have shown that people who have been through a process they regard as fair are more likely to comply with the decision reached by that process than are those who have thought it unfair. Remember when you were a child and felt that your friend was playing unfairly during a game? You abruptly broke off the process, ended your "contract" to play together, and stomped off yelling, "I don't play with cheaters!" As adults, we are a little more civil. When we feel that another has cheated, we silently vow never to play with him again.

A high proportion of defendents in small claims proceedings never pay the judgments ruled against them. However, in a study published in 1984, Craig McEwen and Richard Maiman noted the exceptions. Examining the records of six small claims courts in Maine, the two investigators found that the chances of a defendant paying what the court said he owed were significantly influenced by whether or not he thought he had a fair hearing. This compliance pattern occurred no matter how much the individual was required to pay. People responded to fairness with integrity.

When I want to act fairly I do not merely "see your point of view" or understand how my behavior may affect you. I must also allow myself to be *influenced* by those factors. We are not talking about an intellectual exercise, but, rather, a *commitment to fairness.*

Fairness and Old Hurts

IDEALLY, WE ACT FAIRLY EVEN WHEN THERE IS AN ABSENCE OF CONstraints forcing us to (such as a concrete punishment) or the enticing promise of some reward (such as the approval of others). But when we feel deprived, or insecure, or cheated by life, we find it difficult even to discern what is fair. As a result, our tendency is to *compensate* for those feelings and, in so doing, act unfairly in the moment.

Most of us, as adults, come to relationships with old grievances that get in the way of being rational, acting fairly, and responding to the *present* person and circumstance.

You ask your spouse to call you if he's going to come home late from work so that you don't begin to imagine him in a fiery car wreck. He reacts angrily, "Don't try to control me. I don't want to have to report to you!"

You try to make a reasonable case for why you should be able to go out occasionally with your male friends. She tries to sound jocular, but her hurt at your "rejection" is clear: "Why would you rather spend time with them than me?"

You make an unconscionably high demand to settle a lawsuit you brought against your former business partner because you anticipate that he will try to cheat you out of what is rightfully yours.

Having felt abandoned and rejected as a child twenty-five years ago, you become jealous and angry when your friend offers a coveted invitation to a gala dinner to someone else. You vow never to speak to her again.

I go away for the weekend with my family. My patient, who has always felt unloved, leaves me a message on my answering machine: "If you really cared about me, you would be here when I need you."

All of these individuals hunger for love and fairness from others. Ironically, and tragically, their hurts cause them to react in such an unfair manner that they guarantee they will not receive what they so desperately need. We don't suffer the unreasonableness of others very well. All of us want to be approached with a clean slate, fairly, and not with the history of disappointments that the other brings.

Fairness and Greed

FAIRNESS BECOMES A MOVING TARGET WHEN GREED INTERFERES. WHY do we become greedy? Because we are terrified of not getting enough, of not having enough. Greed is not pretty. We don't aspire to be greedy.

A friend of mine is an investment banker. He puts deals together, finding buyers for sellers. He often begins the process by asking the seller what he wants for his business. After a careful assessment of the assets and liabilities of the company, they arrive at what would be a fair price that the seller could feel good about. Over the years, my friend has recounted numerous tales of a seller being given his price, closing the deal, and then experiencing remorse. Did I miscalculate? he frets. Did I cave in too early? Could I have gotten more? It is easy to lose sight of what is fair when we view the world as an untrustworthy adversary, or a place where I need to squeeze out as much as I can for myself, regardless of any other consideration.

Fairness and Wealth

THE LAST SIX MONTHS OF BULLETINS FROM BAY LAUREL ELEMENTARY School have included a request: Because of the potential danger to children (particularly the younger ones), please do not park your car in the circular driveway of the campus when you arrive for pickup; cars must be parked on the street. Six pleas, six monthly reminders. Yet invariably, when I come for my son, Nathan, I see cars in that circular driveway, driven by individuals who received the same six entreaties as I did. Apparently, these drivers believe that the rule should not apply to them as it does to everyone else. Why aren't these moms and dads bothered by the unfairness of their behavior?

I think it has to do with money. I live in a mostly well-to-do neighborhood where people are used to buying whatever convenience they desire. Parking on the street would be a slight inconvenience, and these parents are not used to going out of their way. Convenience, therefore, has become expected as an inalienable right. I'm sure that these affluent dads and moms are not even aware of their unfairness, as they pass all those cars parked where they were supposed to be. Feelings of entitlement obscure our sense of fairness.

Fairness Subverted

HANDICAPPED PARKING HAS OPENED UP A CAN OF WORMS. I REMEMBER when it was first implemented. I thought, Great. It seemed an idea that sprang from our higher, altruistic self. Let those who are hobbled come first. It is easier for me to walk farther because I am not burdened by any impediment. Handicapped parking was a fair idea. It was an idea that lifted the impaired so that the playing field would become a level one.

My admiration has given way to anger. I am angry because a noble sentiment that reflects the best in us is being abused. How many times have you and I seen a perfectly healthy, able individual emerge from his car parked in that space defined by blue?

A headline in the *Los Angeles Times* read, "DMV Investigators Allege Illegal Use of Disabled Placards." The article began:

> Those trying to find a place to park in upscale Brentwood often feel handicapped. Too many cars always seem to be competing for too few parking spaces outside gourmet coffee outlets and glitzy boutiques.
>
> Motorists on San Vicente Boulevard have had a reason to feel that way, authorities said Friday.
>
> Department of Motor Vehicles investigators said they have observed valet parking attendants used by one of the Westside's trendiest restaurants displaying unauthorized handicapped parking placards to get convenient—and free—parking for customers' cars.
>
> After watching valets outside the Toscana Restaurant stick blue placards in a Porsche and a BMW, state agents nabbed a parking attendant who had pulled a handicapped sign from beneath his shirt and slapped it on the dash of a Mercedes, said Cmdr. Vito Scattaglia of the DMV.

Why am I so bothered? Why can't I just shrug it off? It's more than that voice inside saying, "That's not fair!" It is a hurt, frightened, and disappointed plea: Why do you have to remind me of the selfishness that lurks within? Why do you nourish my cynicism?

"We Are Not All Equal."

I WAS SPEAKING WITH A FRIEND ABOUT ONE OF LIFE'S OBVIOUS IN-equities: the very different manner in which we treat attractive as opposed to homely women. It is not an exaggeration to say that attractive women and homely women live in two different worlds, the former in a world of privilege, the latter in a world of indifference. I lamented the blatant unfairness of it all, the luck of genetic inheritance.

"But all of us are *not* equal," he replied. "Some of us are smarter than others, some of us are more athletic than others. Why shouldn't those people be rewarded for their excellence?"

My friend is certainly correct when he says we are not equal. Some of us are more intelligent than others. Some of us are more perceptive than others. Some of us are more beautiful than others. Some of us are more creative than others.

But smarter people should not be *treated* more kindly than you or me. Athletes should not be treated more sensitively than you or me. Aesthetically pleasing people should not be treated more gratuitously than you or me. Yes, excellence should be rewarded. But winning a Nobel prize should not be cause for being treated with greater human consideration than is extended to any of us.

I'm a Good Person and You're Not

WE DON'T LEVEL THE PLAYING FIELD IN OUR JUDGMENTS OF EACH other.

Imagine you are a new student at the university. You enter the elevator at the Social Sciences building, and as it ascends, you inquire of me, a faculty member, "Do you happen to know where I could find Professor Albert's office?"

"No," I abruptly reply.

You persist, "Any idea where the sociology department might be?"

"No, I don't!" I tersely answer. The elevator door opens on the third floor, we emerge and walk our separate ways. What an unkind son-of-a-bitch, you think.

Now, imagine that I am that new student and you are the faculty member. As the elevator in the Social Sciences building ascends, I inquire, "Do you happen to know where I could find Professor Albert's office?"

"No," you abruptly reply.

I persist, "Any idea where the sociology department might be?"

"No, I don't!" you tersely answer. The elevator door opens on the third floor, we emerge and walk our separate ways. What an unkind son-of-a-bitch, I think.

But in the second case, you hardly see it that way. Instead, you remind yourself of accumulated woes that caused you to act as you did: I would have been more considerate if I didn't have that flat tire on the way in, if I hadn't discovered this morning that my accountant's bad advice cost me thousands of dollars, if I hadn't been informed an hour ago that my grant application that consumed so much of my efforts last year was rejected. No, you don't see yourself as a son-of-a-bitch. Rather, you see yourself as a basically good person who is having a very bad day.

Attribution Theory explains this unfairness in judgment. We not only see others more simply than we see ourselves, but more important, we attribute their unworthy behavior to an internal disposition, to their basic character. That's the kind of person he is, we believe. We explain our own inconsiderateness, on the other hand, by pointing to external pressures and influences, thus retaining a positive self-perception. That wasn't the real me, we reassure ourselves.

Attribution Theory describes a powerful predilection we have for unfairness in our perceptions. We pass judgment on others in hopes of controlling their selfishness so that we can feel safer. We withhold judgment of ourselves in order to promote our own interests and excuse our transgressions. The knowledge of this distorted tendency demands that we give another the benefit of the doubt, that we give him the same leeway that we give ourselves.

Get It in Writing

BY NOW, WE HAVE ALL BEEN ADMONISHED, "READ THE FINE PRINT." Whether it be for a washing machine or an airline ticket, we assume they are offering what they advertise. And then we find out about all of the "exclusions." The promise is diluted. Trust has been further chipped away.

There is an even more harmful variation of "Read the fine print." "Get it in writing." There was a time when you could simply trust another's word. A handshake sealed our promises to one another. The negotiations were over, the deal was done, you drank a toast to the reciprocal benefit that would befall both parties. It felt good. It felt fair. I could turn my back and securely walk away. But now, when I tell my friend (who happens to be a lawyer) about the agreement I just concluded, his immediate response is, "Did you get it in writing?"

Unfortunately, my friend has all too often experienced what you and I have, as well. Old hurts—feelings of deprivation, feelings of having been taken advantage of—get in the way. Six months later, the other party remembers your conversation differently. No, that's not what I said. Or, with even more indignation, "I never would have agreed to that!"

A further word about negotiations. Usually, when we are involved in such a give-and-take occasion, we begin with the anticipation of having to haggle. "I'll come in very low because I know he'll come in too high." We begin with mistrust. Instead, leave your past grievances (probably having nothing to do with me) at the door. Simply approach with a *fair* offer. Let us be partners in justice, and not combatants trying to beat (or beat up on) one another.

The emphasis on the written agreement has also subtly eroded our motivation to keep verbal promises. "Perhaps I said that, but after thinking about it more, I don't really want to do it." We now are comfortable negating a previous promise with the reassuring thought: I know I said that, but I have the right to change my mind. Once again, the focus is simply on *yourself* and not your responsibility to others, your obligation to fairness.

We make marriage *vows*, but then excuse our breaking of those commitments because of fleeting feelings or momentary impulses. "I was just feeling so frustrated and unloved. And here, this new man was being so attentive and flattering. I guess I got carried away." The male variation is often something like, "She was just so beautiful, and it was not going to get complicated. No man could have been expected not to take advantage of that opportunity." Our vows and promises so easily turn to dust.

"Get it in writing" is a frightening way to live. When we emphasize the primacy of the written word, we imply its precedence over *the spirit of fairness*. We imply a recognition of our potential weaknesses that may strike out at a later moment. Get it in writing in case the other individual has a lapse in memory produced by emotional coercion. Moreover, those pressures often have nothing to do with the particular arrangement between the two of you. Perhaps his other ventures have gone sour and he is, therefore, feeling an urgency to squeeze out what he can from you. Regardless, those undermining emotions must be tamed. Commitments must be kept.

Does this sound familiar? Two months ago, you made plans to get together with Fred and Pamela. They are acquaintances, people you don't see frequently because they are a bit boring, although certainly nice enough. Three days before the planned engagement, the telephone rings and you receive an invitation to what sounds like an incredibly interesting, entertaining dinner party. What do you do?

Many of us resort to lying, with some variation of, "I seem to have come down with the flu." Unfortunately, the excuse is often transparent. Or the truth somehow gets back to Fred and Pamela as they run into other people who also attended that dinner party. Put yourself in Fred and Pamela's shoes. Remember when you were growing up and Randy or Melissa chose to play with Steve or Sherry, rather than you? Rejection cuts deeply, whether we are eight or forty-eight.

Commitments must be kept, but some commitments need not be made in the first place. How often have we sighed, or strained to put on a happy face when we have gotten together with people because it was expected of us, because it was politic to do so, or because we were reluctant to offend some rule of etiquette? See whom you want to see. You are not doing anyone a favor by meeting with them for all the wrong reasons. Would you want anyone to socialize with you under the influence of those less than genuine sentiments? Would you want anyone inviting you over solely out of a sense of obligation? Probably not.

Money also gets in the way of keeping commitments. With some exceptions, I have observed that the more money a person has, the more permission he gives himself to break commitments. Money is power, and power induces arrogance. Money also provides a lifestyle of being able to satisfy whims. (At the last minute, you feel like going to that trendy restaurant where reservations are required weeks in advance? No problem. Slip a fifty-dollar bill to the maître d'. Go to the head of the line. The "plain folk" will just have to follow the rules and wait patiently.) Keeping commitments is antithetical to doing whatever one feels like at the moment. The richer you are, the more likely you are to view any restraints as an anathema.

When you make commitments that you don't keep, you offend my desire for fairness. I *want* to believe in you. I want to live my life reassured that the world is filled with trustworthy people. I want to live my life with my guard down.

We need not be rigid about anything, including commitments.

Let's say Mr. Jones borrows ten thousand dollars from you and provides his home as collateral. He agrees to repay the sum in five years. At the five-year deadline, Mr. Jones's business has an unexpected downturn. He needs an extension of six months. You are terribly disappointed because you had planned on buying a new car with that money and had been looking forward to this day for a long time. It is true that, contractually, you could possess Mr. Jones's home and recoup your money. But it wouldn't be fair.

Always balance justice and compassion. And after you have balanced them, add an extra measure of the latter.

Promises

WE ALL BREAK PROMISES, BOTH TO OURSELVES ("I PROMISE TO FIND more balance between work and family," "I promise to lose ten pounds," "I promise to go easier on myself and not be so self-critical," "I promise to lighten up and enjoy life more," "I promise to be more generous") and to others ("I promise I'll be there on time," "I promise I'll come to all your ballet recitals," "I promise I'll be more sensitive to your feelings," "I promise I'll get that report to you on Thursday," "I promise I won't have any more affairs"). Most of the time, we mean those promises when we make them. Our intentions are good. But sometimes, even though I *really* want to keep that promise, my will falters, or my priorities are knocked askew, or my insecurities hold sway.

Try not to make promises you may not be able to keep. Make promises more sparingly. Remember when you were a child and your parent promised, "I'll be at your game," or "I'll make it to your recital," or "I'm sure I'll be back from my business trip for your birthday," or "I promise I'll never embarrass you in front of your friends again." And remember how hurt you were when your father or mother let you down? That's the way it still feels as an adult, particularly when a loved one breaks a promise. Why are you doing this to me? Why can't I count on you? you plead.

What Are Reasonable Expectations of Others?

WOULD YOU WANT OTHERS TO JUDGE YOU AS HARSHLY AS YOU JUDGE them?

When you have been treated inconsiderately, when you have observed rudeness, when you have witnessed a public outburst of anger at a family member, when you have seen someone cut into a line, you have probably thought, "How could she do that?" But are there no circumstances under which you could imagine acting in that manner?

It is the personal affront that stings acutely and produces our most bitter reaction. Why didn't you invite me to your birthday party? Why didn't you acknowledge my help on your project? Why did you say those things about me to Charley? Why did you walk past me and act as if I weren't even there? Families torn apart, close friendships severed, and we often can no longer even remember the cause of our condemnation. For the moment, however, let us assume that the memory of that hurt has seared your psyche.

"Why did you sever that relationship?" I ask.

"Because he———," you hurl back at me.

"Because of *that* you ended a relationship with someone you love?"

I might pursue you even further. "Did you ever consider *why* he acted that way? Did you ever wonder about the hurts that drove him?"

And finally, "Wouldn't *you* have wanted him to consider those last two questions before he cut you off?"

You might reply to my challenge, "I don't care why he did it. All I know is that he hurt me deeply."

And I would venture, "But you *do* care about his absence."

When you rip someone out of your life who meant a great deal, *you* have lost.

We will *inevitably* be hurt and disappointed by those we love. We want to assume that they will always treat us with kindness and generosity. We want to be able to trust that they will forever treat us fairly. But they won't. Last year, I had to conduct a business transaction with one of my best friends, a man whom I have known for twenty years. At one point in the negotiation, I believed he was being less than candid with me. I felt cheated. More devastatingly, I felt the pain of a child who had been mistreated by someone who was *always* supposed to love him. I told my friend how hurt I felt. But then I added, "I won't let this ruin our relationship. For me, our friendship is a marriage. We will undoubtedly hurt each other. But I won't walk away."

A few people are truly evil, and their actions are unforgivable. Most of us, however, are simply flawed. Everyone is fighting a battle against his fears, hurts, and insecurities so that his goodness can emerge. In *How Good Do We Have to Be?*, Harold Kushner exhorts us to be more tolerant and accepting. He also reminds us to be realistic:

We too have the power to choose happiness over righteousness. Righteousness means remembering every time someone hurt us or disappointed us, and never letting them forget it (and— frightening thought—giving them the right to remember every time we hurt them or let them down and constantly remind us of it). Happiness means giving people the right to be human, to be weak and selfish and occasionally forgetful, and realizing that we have no alternative to living with imperfect people. (I once saw a button that read, "Never attribute to malice what can be explained by stupidity." I might emend that to read,

"Never attribute to malice what can be explained by human frailty and imperfection.")

"If you treat me fairly, I will treat you fairly." Sounds like a reasonable, straightforward way to live. But Rabbi Stewart Vogel of Temple Aliyah in Woodland Hills, California, explained the pact's defect. "Let's say I ask my neighbor to borrow his garden hose, and he refuses. The next week, he has need of my garden hose and approaches me. I will give it to him. The issue is that I won't let other people's behavior interfere with my acting as I should."

Stewart Vogel implies that all of us simply *deserve* to be treated fairly. Furthermore, "getting back at you" only harms me, for I then obscure my higher, moral self. Instead of experiencing the freedom to do good, I withdraw into my "every man for himself" bunker. When I forfeit my generosity and decency, I am only left with cynicism.

It is a difficult trick, but one that you can master. Do not let another's behavior deprive you of your impulse to do what's right.

Do People Get What They Deserve?

LIFE IS NOT FAIR. WE ALL KNOW THAT. RABBI HAROLD KUSHNER IS A believer in God and in the goodness of the world. At the age of three, Rabbi Kushner's bright, happy son, Aaron, was diagnosed with a condition called progeria, "rapid aging." Harold and his wife were told by the pediatrician that "Aaron would never grow much beyond three feet in height, would have no hair on his head or body, would look like a little old man while he was still a child, and would die in his early teens." Aaron died two days after his fourteenth birthday.

Consumed with Aaron's fate, as well as his own, Rabbi Kushner responded to his son's death with *When Bad Things Happen to Good People,* an attempt to make sense of why the innocent suffer.

It is a question that bothers and baffles all of us who are sensitive to human pain. It is a question that certainly touches on the issue of fairness. Why me? I don't deserve to suffer. And I certainly don't deserve to suffer more than Jim or Michael or Sally or Margie.

On more than one occasion while I was growing up, my father reminded me, "Everybody has their *pekele*. (*Pekele* is a Yiddish word that literally means "package," but in this figurative context means "burden.") We know most people only by their wrapping. "How are you?" "Fine." While all looks in place on the outside, we never learn about his financial ruin, his impotence due to a diabetic condition, her insomnia, her mastectomy, their inability to naturally conceive, or their fifteen-year-old son who is a drug addict, and their thirteen-year-old daughter who still wets her bed. It is important to remember that you have not been unfairly singled out for heartache. Everyone has their *pekele*.

You might still insist, "My burden is greater than yours." But how do we measure suffering? If my thirteen-year-old daughter still wets her bed, and your bright, fifteen-year-old son is getting D's in school because he refuses to apply himself, whose pain is greater? If I have lost all of my savings because I was duped into a fraudulent scheme, and you have been told that you will have to relocate to another city (and leave your lifelong friends and extended family) if you want to retain your job, who experiences more heartache?

Don't get caught up in measurement and comparison. Aside from my trivial difficulties (such as my car breakdown, my leaky roof), I simply deserve your empathy and concern when life confronts me with painful challenges. Of course, some troubles should immediately command your compassion: the loss of loved ones, serious physical illness or disability, a child's self-destructive behavior, and financial disaster (not only because it feels like it threatens my very physical existence, but also because it so affects my sense of dignity), to name only a few.

When all is said and done, are burdens or rewards evenly distributed? Harold Kushner's question, "Why do the innocent suffer?" implies a related puzzle: Do people get what they deserve? In Chapter Three, we saw how our need to feel secure, as well as morally superior, drives us to assume that another's misfortune was somehow caused by his own actions. Ironically, however, in order to maintain my positive self-image, I arrive at a completely different explanation for my misfortune. "I got screwed. I was just minding my own business, doing what I was supposed to do, and I got screwed." Or, "I guess I'm just not a very lucky person." (The exception is the depressed individual. He thinks: "I'm worthless, so it's not surprising that misfortune befalls me.")

To know that not only do bad things happen to good people, but that good things happen to bad people, deeply offends our sensibilities and desire for fairness. So we try to salve our wound with bromides. For the former, we offer: "There must be a reason. It's part of a larger plan." For the latter, we submit: "Don't worry, what goes around, comes around," or "He'll get his in another life."

The Terror of Randomness

IT IS NOT ONLY UNFAIRNESS THAT RANKLES. THE SEEMING RANDOM-ness of outcomes shakes our core as well. That's why we are superstitious. Maintaining superstitions is an attempt to reassure ourselves that fortune or misfortune are not haphazard and arbitrary. If we can only grasp cause-effect relationships, we will be able to control our world. So the basketball coach, whose team wins for the first time in two years, vows, "I'll wear these orange socks I have on tonight at every game!" A five-year-old child jumps over the cracks in the sidewalk so that monsters will not devour him.

(The reverse process occurs just as readily. When we believe that whatever we might do will prove inconsequential, we become passive and depressed. We essentially give up.)

If there is a rhyme and reason, if there are underlying principles governing life's outcomes, then I won't feel so vulnerable. If I can only make sense of what has occurred, I will feel safer. But our inability to accept the randomness of life can lead us astray.

Robert Marks, a forty-two-year-old attorney, was tearing himself apart. His sixteen-year-old daughter, Tamara, had been killed in a car accident the previous year. "She was too young to drive. I knew it. How could I have let this sixteen-year-old drive? We fought about it. 'All my friends are driving!' she yelled at me. So, at some point, I gave in. . . . Against my better judgment. . . . Why didn't I put my foot down? . . . Why wasn't I a responsible father?" In Robert's attempt to find a reason for Tamara's death, he found an apparent, but unwarranted explanation—that he wasn't a good enough, protective enough parent.

In reality, Robert did all he could, under the circumstances. He fought for what he believed was best for his daughter. But all parents have "given in" to a teenager's insistence about an issue that felt like life-and-death to her. Robert must tell himself that he did his best to balance his responsibility as a father with his compassion for his daughter's yearnings to be independent and feel accepted by her friends.

Freddie Cohen is a child, but he made the same mistake as Robert. In trying to make sense of events, he drew unwarranted and self-destructive conclusions. Freddie was eight years old when his father moved out of the house to separate from Freddie's mother. During our first session, Freddie, looking down at the carpet, spoke in a barely audible voice: "I know why my dad left. I'm no good, and he got fed up with me. If I wasn't so bad all the time, he and my mom would still be together. . . . Everybody's going to leave me . . . I know it. . . . I'm just no good."

Children of divorce commonly worry that they were, in some way, instrumental in causing the insurmountable difficulties that led to the breakup. For example, if parents had openly and severely disagreed about child-rearing approaches ("You spoil him too much!" "Stop being so mean to her!"), a son or daughter may latch on to this evidence as proof of his or her responsibility for the parents' irreconcilable differences. (Even in situations where marital conflict is hidden behind closed bedroom doors, children often assume blame for the divorce. They grasp at straws. If only I had *somehow* been a better boy, this would not have happened, he believes.) Perhaps a child learned that he was never wanted by one parent and that this disagreement caused considerable tension. Or, as was the case with Freddie, a child gets into some trouble and perceives the subsequent departure of a parent as a rejection of him. Freddie searched for explanations and unrealistically found them in his own perceived shortcomings.

Why Do Some People Have All the Luck?

"WHY DO SOME PEOPLE HAVE ALL THE LUCK?" WE WONDER, USUALLY enviously. (In fact, we are once again crying out, "It's not fair!") I don't know the answer to that question. Oftentimes, however, what appears to be blind luck is the careful preparation of the right ingredients that had been gestating for a long period of time. It's the old story: "I've been rehearsing for thirty years to become an overnight success." Another answer to the vexing question "Why do some people have all the luck?" may lie in certain characteristics that you have and I don't. I was speaking with my friend Murray about his phenomenal success in the stock market during the past few years. I was lamenting the fact that I had missed the tremendous run-up in equities that had recently taken place. He pointed out, "Aaron, you're just not a risk-taker, and the stock market is always a gamble." Murray isn't simply lucky. He is the kind of person who is willing to put his money on the line, and I'm not.

Many people don't get what they deserve. Rabbi Joel Rembaum

of Temple Beth Am emphasizes to me that, "God has made an imperfect world, and it is our job to perfect it." In his office at the Archdiocese, Father Gregory Coiro tells me, "You can't have love without justice, and the most important expression of love is charity." Charity is our way of making the world a bit more fair. Giving to charity provides another important function as well: It makes me aware that there are many who are much less fortunate than me. It produces a seismic shift in my perspective, from "Other people have all the luck," to "I'm a very fortunate guy."

There are many things—too many things—in life that we cannot control. I think of the writer Ann Beattie's fruitless desire to safekeep her children:

Do everything right, all the time, and the child will prosper. It's as simple as that, except for fate, luck, heredity, chance, and the astrological sign under which the child was born, his order of birth, his first encounter with evil, the girl who jilts him in spite of his excellent qualities, the war that is being fought when he is a young man, the drugs he may try once or too many times, the friends he makes, how he scores on tests, how well he endures kidding about his shortcomings, how ambitious he becomes, how far he falls behind, circumstantial evidence, ironic perspective, danger when it's least expected, difficulty in triumphing over circumstance, people with hidden agendas, and animals with rabies.

No, life is not always fair. But, you and I can *be* fair. No matter how tightly we try to hold on to the steering wheel, unexpected and uncontrollable storms will buffet us about. We can't always prevent illness, accidents, or financial disasters. But we can *choose* how we live and, by our example, encourage others as well.

A *few challenges:*

The next time the checkout person forgets to charge you for an item, point it out to him or her.

In the coming week, choose a charity whose work you admire and make a donation.

Do something generous or considerate for someone who has treated you inconsiderately.

CHAPTER FIVE

Duty

SOMEHOW, WE HAVE COME TO A POINT WHERE we believe we should be able to do whatever we want. We rebel against any attempts to limit our choices. Obligation feels like the antithesis of freedom. To invoke "moral demands" is perceived by many to be a form of coercion.

Being a moral person, doing what's right, implies the fulfillment of duties. Many of us give to charity because "it's a good tax write-off, and it helps people, anyway." When those who can contribute refuse to be charitable, we shrug our shoulders and again invoke the notion of individual freedom: "It's a personal decision." It is noteworthy that nowhere in the Bible is there mention of individual rights. There is, however, a great deal of direction for how we are obliged to behave toward others.

It is my duty to reach out and share my good fortune. I know that the word *obligation* feels so heavy, so onerous to many of you. But charity, for example, is a positive obligation. Furthermore, *it is an obligation fulfilled not only for others, but for your higher self.* And you do it because that's what a good person does.

Regrettably, most of my colleagues in the mental health community have emphasized the need for self-love and have neglected the value of acknowledging obligations to others. Psychologists want their clients to feel good about themselves. They provide what they refer to as "unconditional positive regard." No matter how you behave, you must still feel you are okay. They urge their clients to reject the mores and demands of the external world and, instead, find a standard with which they can feel *comfortable*. Psychologists, unfortunately, are not big on obligations.

It would be great if what made you happy also coincided with doing good deeds for others. But we are often feeling too selfish, too frightened, too insecure, too jealous, or too deprived to act from our generous self. And because we can't rely on our feelings to do what's right, we have duties.

Even when our feelings are laudable ones, we can't count on them. How many of us have felt deeply, cared deeply about the starving children of Rwanda, the children who grow up in fatherless homes, or the children who are stricken with leukemia? How many of us have *done* anything to alleviate their suffering?

Unfortunately, if we care deeply enough, we feel noble and *satisfied*. We have already demonstrated our compassionate character and concern for others.

Think of it. How many people do you know who actually call on the sick, visit the lonely, or serve Thanksgiving dinner at a shelter? We are obligated to make financial contributions, if we can. But when we only write a check, we lose the recognition of our connectedness to others, we lose the awareness of our good fortune, we lose the opportunity to provide human comfort by holding a hand and offering a smile, or a tear.

Reverend Cecil Murray is clear about the duty to care. He also refuses to place his trust in natural feelings. "We love those who are closest to us because of a certain chemistry. *But genuine love is an act of will.*"

The technical name for the branch of ethics dealing with obligations is deontology. Immanuel Kant was a deontologist in that he placed moral obligations at the very center of his ethics: "I ought, therefore I am." In *The Fundamental Principles of the Metaphysic of Ethics*, Kant wrote, "Worries and unsatisfied wants may easily become a great temptation to the transgression of duties." For Kant, moral actions must be prompted by a sense of duty, and not rely on fleeting inclinations. Furthermore, the dictates of duty insure that even those without empathy for the pain of others will act in a moral fashion.

We live in a culture that extols the virtue of individualism. It feeds our tendency to feel, "It's every man for himself." Indeed, we experience a keen sense of obligation to ourself and to our immediate family. "Life's tough," I hear you say. "It's all I can do to take care of my own."

We also encourage our children to excel over others, to implicitly distance themselves from others. In contrast, certain societies in Africa and Asia teach the value of interdependence and community. And across cultures, studies routinely uncover greater competitiveness and a more selfish orientation in children who live in the city as opposed to the country. While we exhort our children to "Be the best you can be," we forget to teach them about their responsibilities to others.

We need to counteract "rights talk." We need to feel connected to our neighbors, our colleagues, our acquaintances, and the stranger. We need to feel the continuity between those who came before us and those who will come after. We need to feel a part of a larger whole. We need to sense the invisible ties that bind us to one another.

Our sense of disconnectedness is starkly manifested in the incredibly low turnout rate during elections. Far fewer than fifty percent of us bother to choose our President. In local elections, where one might imagine turnout would be high because the stakes are closer to home, it is not unusual for only one in five to bother casting a ballot. I am not a part of the polity, we feel. I'll just take care of myself.

Rabbi Harold Schulweis visits the sick, counsels the troubled, and champions the underdog. That's part of his job description. But on a personal level, he is acutely aware of his connectedness to those beyond him, and the responsibilities those ties entail. When I asked, "How do you control your immoral impulses?" he surprised me by one of his responses. "I'm a public figure. If I did something immoral, people would generalize my behavior to the entire Jewish people." For Rabbi Schulweis, his own morality is not simply a private affair, or an expression of his higher self. He remembers that his behavior has consequences for millions of others. Imagine if we would all monitor our own behavior with the thought: I can't do that because of what people might think about all white people (or black people, or brown people, or Catholics, or Jews, or women, or men, etc.).

When discussion turns to our obligations to others, we often give single people a free ride. We demand less of single people. We say that marriage and children mature you, and it is at that point that you must become a responsible person. But single men and women have obligations to many people—friends, neighbors, coworkers, and those less fortunate, to name a few.

We know singles who continue to have difficulty making a lifelong commitment to a mate, even when they are thirty or forty years old. We understand their fears of intimacy, their attempts to avoid abandonment, their inability to give up control. While many singles demonstrate their social conscience, some, however, refuse to take on *any* responsibilities to others that might curtail their freedom. And we excuse their behavior as a "lack of maturity," instead of summoning them to fulfill their duties.

The Obligation to Care

CARING IS MORE THAN A FEELING. CARING DEMANDS ACTION. HOW many times have I sat across from a couple and heard the wife complain to her husband, "I don't feel loved by you."

His response is usually, "But you know I love you."

Then I ask, "What do you do to show her that you love her?"

He is quick to point out, "Well, I work hard. I take care of her. We have a nice lifestyle. She never wants for anything."

I don't let him off so easily, however. "But what do you do that says to her how *special* she is to you?"

It's not enough that we know our husband or wife cares about us. We know he or she cares about a lot of people. What we clamor for is to feel *special*. And that can only occur when you *demonstrate* that I am special to you. Doing what you ordinarily do in life is, in most cases, insufficient. I want you to go out of your way.

We care by deciding to be sensitive to another's feelings, even when self-interest would urge us otherwise. There is a law in the Talmud that states that you are not permitted to ask a shopkeeper the price of an item if you know that you will not purchase it. You are certainly allowed to comparison shop. But, for example, if you know that a store has advertised to beat any price in town, you are not allowed to go to various stores simply to find out the price of an item so that you can inevitably go elsewhere. You cannot raise someone's hopes under false pretenses. Imagine if you were the shopkeeper and someone came in, asked you questions about the camera in your display counter, and admitted, "I'm here because the store down the block offered to beat anyone's price. I really came in only to find out what you charge." We have a duty to not create *unnecessary* disappointment.

We often mislead others about our romantic intentions, as well, although men are more frequent culprits than women. Men understand what my friend, Ellen, revealed to me some time ago. In doing research for one of my previous books, I asked Ellen, a single, thirty-one-year-old photographer, if she had to be in love with a man before she went to bed with him. "I don't have to be in love with him," she replied. "But I have to sense that there is the possibility of this *becoming* a romantic relationship."

Some women, of course, kid themselves. They believe they are in love in order to give themselves permission to engage in sexual relations. But most are like Ellen. In order to move forward sexually, they need to believe in the possibility of commitment. Having figured this out, most men are unwilling to flatly state (when it is true), "I am only interested in using your body." But in this case, caring demands honesty. To extend the shopkeeper analogy, men should not casually explore the contours of the item if there is no genuine interest in following through. We will encounter enough inevitable disappointments in life. Let's not generate unnecessary ones.

"Hi. How Are You?"

WHICH BRINGS ME TO:
   "Hi. How are you?"
   "Fine. How are you?"
   "Great."

The above interaction occurs millions of times every day. Moreover, seldom does a day go by without your complicity in this "dishonesty." Most of the time, everything is not "fine" with you or me. Seldom do we feel "great." Yet, we persist in our dishonesty without a twinge of compunction. But there are repercussions.

This seemingly innocuous dishonesty produces estrangement. For, on many levels, we experience anger at not feeling allowed to be more forthcoming, hurt at the knowledge that the other does not truly care about our well-being, and an underlying wariness as our belief in the potential for dishonesty in our fellow human being is further confirmed. When I perceive your caring to be phony, I lose faith in your ability to truly care. And that perception makes me feel more isolated and alone.

At the same time, such dishonest interactions "grease the wheels" of human intercourse, allowing a certain ease, a superficiality that feels safer, and a semblance of caring. But I resent the fact that dishonesty appears to be *demanded* of me by social convention. When I, too, respond "Fine," I acknowledge that our interaction is a game, a dance, and not a truly human, caring encounter.

Why don't we tell each other how we really feel? Indeed, I may not want to disclose my problems to you because we are only superficial acquaintances. I have a right to privacy and the choice of who will become familiar with my personal life.

But there is a deeper reason, as well. If I tell you how I really feel, you won't like me as much. You will see me as weak, or neurotic, or less than "together." I will feel vulnerable because you have not dropped your armor while I have exposed my underside. The advantage in this "every person for himself" world would now be yours. In most cases, it is *fear* that causes us to lie.

Our emphasis on individualism has fueled our everyday dishonesties. When there is a greater sense of community, we believe the other does care and wants to help in any way he can. We are, therefore, more likely to expose our difficulties without fear of rejection or attack.

If you don't really care about how I am, just say, "Hello." But, if you do care, I'd like to know that I can speak about my financial investment that turned to disaster, my heartache over my daughter's choice of fiancé, or my fear of the results of the biopsy that I underwent this morning. It would provide me great comfort to know that I could share any of that with you.

The Waiter

MY FRIEND GEORGE CALLED ME EXCITEDLY AFTER HIS FIRST DATE with Melanie. "She's great! She's intelligent, gorgeous, and laughs in all the right places. This could be the one." Then, George called a week later. "Melanie and I are history."

"What happened?" I asked with astonishment.

"We went out to dinner Wednesday night, and that's where it ended," he said. "Oh, she was sweet and charming with me. But you should have seen how she treated the waiter! She was rude, obnoxious, demanding. She treated him as if he weren't human." George understands how to evaluate character.

How do you treat those to whom you do not feel *obliged* to act considerately? How do you treat those from whom you don't want or need anything? How do you treat those who have no power over you? How do you treat even those who are close to you, when no one is around to observe?

"It's Your Life."

HOW MANY TIMES HAVE YOU SEEN SOMEONE YOU CARE ABOUT ON THE verge of making a big mistake? Whether it be choosing whom to fall in love with, presenting unreasonable demands to another, leaving a satisfying job for a promise that will never materialize, or severing a valuable relationship, we can see disaster coming, and we fail to say anything. Or, we begin to say something, are cut off with, "That's what I want to do!" and quickly accede, "It's your life."

We can't always stop someone when he is determined to act. But we have a duty to urge, "Let's talk about this. Let's think this through. What might happen if you did that? Are you approaching this realistically? Or, are your wishes and fantasies getting the better of you? How about holding off that decision for a week, and then see if you still feel like doing that?"

When I am unsure of my next step, I run it by a friend whose opinion I respect, and whom I can count on to be objective — neither too soft, nor too hard on me. (I must also believe he doesn't have any vested interest in my ultimate decision.)

It is difficult for many of us to ask for advice. It is uncomfortable to publicly acknowledge our weak spots and, thereby, admit that we cannot possibly be objective about the right thing to do. I am lucky to have one or two precious friends who keep me on the straight and narrow when my insecurities, fears, and resentments might lead me to destructive action. I hope you have someone who can fill that role as well.

Masculine Versus Feminine Morality

WHO IS MORE MORAL, A WOMAN OR A MAN? THE EARLY EXPERIMENTS of psychologist Lawrence Kohlberg, the most influential theoretician of moral development, seemed to indicate that males tended to be more highly developed than females in their abilities to evaluate and justly resolve moral dilemmas. However, in a paper in 1977 that she later expanded into the book *A Different Voice*, Harvard psychologist Carol Gilligan presented an alternative explanation for Kohlberg's findings.

Carol Gilligan believes that men and women focus on different concerns when approaching moral issues. Having a more individualistic and competitive bent, males typically utilize a *justice orientation* when attempting to come to grips with the issue of conflicting rights. Females, on the other hand, are more likely to adopt a *care orientation*. A morality of justice assumes that people's interests often conflict and, therefore, we need objective rules to adjudicate those differences. A morality of care presumes that the welfare of others is intrinsically bound up with one's own well-being. Hence, I am responsible for your happiness, as well as my own. A morality of care implies that I have a duty to acknowledge and respond to your sensibilities. In fact, males and females differ in the *types* of situations that they are apt to *view* as moral dilemmas. Females are more attuned to circumstances that provide conflict inherent in attending to the feelings of others. Males are more likely to notice conflict pertaining to issues of justice and fairness.

Even during infancy, girls orient themselves to attachment and connectedness via their identification with the mother. Having to separate from the mother and form a male identity, boys orient themselves to individualism and disconnectedness. Through their tie to the mother, girls develop a belief in their similarity to others and, therefore, an enhanced ability to empathize. Pushing away from the mother, boys more profoundly experience a sense of differentness from others. An orientation of connectedness requires a sensitivity to people's needs and a certain benevolence. (Carol Gilligan emphasizes that girls are concerned about not hurting.) An orientation to individualism and competitiveness necessitates rules for fairness.

In a classic dilemma designed by Lawrence Kohlberg, a man is desperate to save his wife, who is dying of cancer. A cure is available, but the druggist who controls the drug charges more money than the man has. Should the man steal the drug? Carol Gilligan quotes an example of how differently Amy and Jake reason about this quandary.

> *Interviewer:* Should the man steal the drug?
>
> *Amy:* Well, I don't think so. I think there might be other ways besides stealing it, like if he could borrow the money or make a loan or something, but he really shouldn't steal the drug—but his wife shouldn't die either. If he stole the drug, he might save his wife then, but if he did, he might have to go to jail, and then his wife might get sicker again, and he

couldn't get any more of the drug, and it might not be good. So, they should really just talk it out and find some other ways to make the money.

Jake (explaining his answer that the man, Heinz, should steal the drug): For one thing, a human life is worth more than money, and if the druggist only makes a thousand dollars, he is still going to live, but if Heinz doesn't steal the drug, his wife is going to die. (The interviewer asks, "Why is life worth more than money?") Because the druggist can get a thousand dollars later from rich people with cancer, but Heinz can't get his wife again.

Amy sees the moral dilemma as a "narrative of relationships over time." She assumes that, if people only care enough, they can work through their problems by "talking it out." Jake sees the situation as a "math problem with humans." Jake senses that people must sometimes act on their own, even if they must break some codes of conduct.

In reality, males and females do not orient one way *or* the other. Both sexes use justice and care orientations, although men use the former more vigorously than the latter, and vice versa for females. As traditional roles become more permeable, we would expect even more overlap. For example, when fathers take on increasing responsibilities for the raising of their children, they become more empathic. That enhanced ability to empathize will result in men giving increasing weight to sensibilities rather than rules.

Context can sway gender proclivities. When we look at women who have entered occupations that had previously been dominated by men, they tend to move closer to men in how they evaluate conflict. For example, female lawyers are as developed in their reasoning about justice and rights as their male counterparts. Studies have shown that men and women with similar occupational histories score almost identically on tests of moral judgment. Understandably, therefore, we are likely to see the greatest gender differences in moral orientation when we compare women who have chosen the more traditional household role and men who occupy conventional male positions outside of the home.

In *The Moral Sense*, James Q. Wilson cites another illustration of the influence of context when discussing cultural expectations for interpersonal etiquette. Grace Goodell, an anthropologist who had spent years studying the industrialized nations of the Pacific Rim, suggested to him that, in some respects, the moral thinking of East Asian businessmen resembled that of eleven-year-old Western girls. Wilson wrote:

> For example, East Asian businessmen often manage their commercial relationships with one another in ways that are designed to maintain those relationships more than to assert legal claims, just as Western girls manage their games in ways that keep the game going even at some cost to the rules. In the Asian business world, anyone who emphasizes contractual obligations, legal rights, or formal rules is guilty of a grave breach of etiquette. These executives are competitive, often fiercely so, but the competition is constrained by a moral sense that neither party should embarrass the other, even at some cost in money. Fairness, abstractly conceived, is less important than comity.

Obviously, there must be a balance struck between the ethics of justice and the ethics of caring. Those only concerned with rules and impartiality may make efficient bureaucrats, but at the price of not responding to human needs. As a teacher, I must be willing to consider exceptions when my students have legitimate excuses and, yes, risk the accusation that the criteria I utilize in making those decisions are subjective ones. As a psychotherapist, I must balance the needs of a patient with an appreciation of his duties to others beyond himself.

Of course, justice must not be *suppressed* by our sympathies. The Bible warns against unjust compassion. For example, judges are instructed not to favor poor people over the rich. Nevertheless, the Talmud speaks up about where God's predilection lies: "Even God prays. What is His prayer? 'May it be Thy will that My love of compassion overwhelm My demand for strict justice.' "

Giving Freely

GIVING WITHOUT THE EXPECTATION OF ANYTHING IN RETURN. WHO does that anymore? In its purest form, you offer because you care, because it is your duty, and because I am you and you are me. But our pure impulses have become soiled.

At those times when you do give freely, but are met with my immediate gesture of reciprocity, I have taken something away from you. I have tarnished your impulse to goodness and your assertion that we are in this enterprise together.

We lose sleep when we owe. It is not simply a need to reciprocate that stirs us. Because we are so accustomed to anticipating a quid pro quo somewhere along the line, we have become mistrustful and cynical of those who give. We assume, You have given to me so that I will return a favor in the future.

Giving without any desire or expectation of return is the highest form of giving. But we live in an age of networking. I think to myself, I'll serve on the Board of that charity because it will increase my visibility in the community. It will be good for business.

I attend a breakfast of "Young Professionals" and sit at a table with ten others who are exchanging pleasantries and making introductions. It seems like simple camaraderie. But very soon, we are speaking of "synergy," potential areas where we might mutually benefit. If you determine that I will not be a potential source of referrals, you quickly shift your gaze to the next person. The breakfast ends, we shake hands, and exchange embossed cards with our title engraved.

Best-selling business books remind us, "You never know what the potential of that next contact might be." We no longer have "acquaintances," we have "contacts."

Friendships are not immune to our adherence to reciprocity. "What am I getting out of this relationship?" we often wonder. I remember one individual who said of a ten-year friendship, "I feel *abused*," because he thought he was giving more than he was receiving. We even calculate in marriage. Recently, Michael Daley, a thirty-six-year-old building contractor and father of three boys, came to see me because he wanted to "reevaluate his marriage." "I work my butt off, sixty, seventy hours a week. The stress I'm under is unbelievable. My wife gets to stay at home and take care of the kids. When I walk in the door at night, *she* tells *me* how tired she is! And we hardly have sex anymore. I can't help but think, What am *I* getting out of this marriage?"

I listen to Michael and questions go through my mind. Why do you work seventy hours a week? Why don't you reduce the stress level in your life? Why do you assume raising three boys is like being on perpetual vacation? Why don't you value the fact that your children have their mother so available to them? Why do you simply focus on sex as the currency in which you should be repaid for your efforts? Regardless of the specific questions, Michael, like many spouses, is adding up the credit and debit columns of his marriage. He wants to know what he's getting for his output.

For the sake of fairness, for the sake of individual dignity, it is important that my relationship to you not be one-sided *over the long term*. (Unfortunately, so many of us assess the debits and credits of our relationships on a weekly or monthly basis.) I am only human. If I feel that the scales of giving and taking are radically out of balance, I will, at best, lose interest in you. At worst, I will start to feel deprived and resentful.

Keep in mind that giving can take many forms. It is often apparent that individuals monitor the give-and-take equation in very tangible and concrete ways. My friend Jerry, an attorney, recently told me that he barters with a client. His client, a ticket broker, provides premium seats to athletic events and concerts. Jerry reciprocates with his legal services. But you have also known the inestimable value of having a friend who offers less tangible gifts—a friend who is a "good listener," a friend who you know simply cares.

Try to refrain from calculating, from keeping a strict scorecard. To paraphrase a poem I recently read: Forget what you have done for your friend, or spouse, or child, and remember what they have done for you.

How Complaining Offends

I KNOW A UROLOGIST THROUGH A MUTUAL FRIEND. DURING THE 1980s, before the explosion of HMOs, and when many physicians were at their earning power peak, he had an annual income in the high six figures. In more recent years, he has averaged about three hundred thousand dollars. Since the "leaner" era began, it seems as though every time I run into him at my friend's house, he is holding court about the injustices of the marketplace. "Physicians can't make a decent living now. It's no fun anymore. They're making it impossible for us." Whenever he starts in, I walk away.

I want to be polite, but his remarks are just too unseemly, too insensitive. They reflect such a complete lack of recognition of those who must truly struggle. They indicate this urologist's narrow focus. They imply an absolute failure to identify with humanity, those of us who are mere mortals.

"I've got my own problems," is an often voiced sentiment to justify self-absorption. Indeed, everyone has their *pekele*, everyone has burdens—financial straits, sickness, emotions that paralyze, unreasonably demanding loved ones, catastrophic fears, uncontrollable compulsions, physical handicaps, a bitter marriage, family members on drugs, children who are painfully insecure, or bosses who torment them. But have you noticed, as I have, that oftentimes it is those carrying the greatest personal load who are also the most forthcoming in their offer of assistance to the needy? These individuals are overwhelmed. However, their sense of duty compels them to care for others as well as "their own."

What can keep us from complaining? Perspective.

Unfortunately, it often takes illness to produce that perspective, to formulate that necessary question, What's *really* important? For most of life's obstacles, it is useful to remind myself, "This, too, shall pass."

I get crazed about ants. Periodically, I wake up in the morning to an ant infestation in our house. Thousands of ants in the pantry, in the closets, and under the sink. Sometimes I can't even see where they are coming from. I feel that my life is out of my control. I go nuts. It helps when my wife, Rebecca, points out, "Honey, it's ants. It's not cancer."

Don't misunderstand me. I am all for talking about personal concerns with others who care. When I am in psychological or physical pain, I need someone to listen, to sympathize, and perhaps provide guidance. But gratuitous complaining obscures for all of us what is really important in life. In the case of my urologist acquaintance, his complaints of financial hardship produce a divide between him and the ninety-five percent of average individuals. "That's a hardship?" we gasp incredulously.

Imagine the following: We run into each other in the parking lot and I go on and on about my ant problem, or my car that stalled and had to be towed again, or my favorite toy that broke, or my five-hour flight delay, or my suit that was ruined by the cleaners.

And during all the time that I prattle on, you keep hearing the words spoken earlier in the week by your doctor, "You're going to need a mastectomy."

It is my duty to be sensitive to the weight of your load. It behooves me, therefore, to *anticipate* the possibility that my complaining might offend you. When you are experiencing a serious difficulty and I relate my ant problem or car deficiency, you will withdraw. If I complain about my income having been reduced from five-hundred-thousand to three-hundred-thousand dollars a year, while you are struggling to make ends meet, you will feel hopeless and enraged. In both cases, you will experience me as so different from you, caught up in my trivia, while your life feels like it is falling apart. Instead of feeling cared about, you will feel even more isolated and oppressed.

We have a duty not to complain. When we refrain, we will all have the opening to share life's true tests with one another and, thereby, ease our personal burden.

Your Responsibilities to Your Children

AS SELF-CENTERED AS I CAN SOMETIMES BE, IF SOMEONE WERE POINTing a gun at both myself and my child and told me to choose who would be killed, it would take less than a second for me to answer. I know how deeply you care about your children as well.

And yet, as parents, we don't necessarily give our children what we should. I am not, here, referring to fathers who desert their children (or their pregnant mate even before the child is born). I am not referring to drug-addicted mothers who lose sight of their duty to nurture because of their fog-inducing habit. I am referring to you and me, parents with the best of intentions, parents who want to be involved with their children, parents who want to do what's right.

I began my book *The Gift of Fatherhood* with the following:

Despite all the developmental theories I had digested, despite my extensive training as a clinical psychologist, despite all the patients I had seen over the years, I was unprepared for what fatherhood really meant until I had my own children.

I was unprepared for the overwhelming feelings of love and protectiveness I would feel toward my children.

I was unprepared for the energy my children would require of me.

I was unprepared for the ambivalence I would feel about their presence.

I was unprepared for the ongoing demands they would make upon me.

I was unprepared for the ensuing, continuous struggle to find a balance in my life.

I was unprepared for how the importance of family would change my life perspective forever.

I was unprepared for how much pleasure my children would give me.

I was unprepared for how anxious and frightened I would feel about them.

I was unprepared for the profound changes which would take place in my marriage after my children were born.

I would now add: I did not fully appreciate the moral duty I had to my children.

We have the awesome opportunity and responsibility to nurture and shape our unformed sons and daughters. Our duties to them are of paramount importance.

YOU HAVE THE DUTY TO SPEND MORE TIME WITH YOUR CHILDREN.

Your children require your presence. The more time you spend with your children, the more attuned you will be to their abilities. The more time you spend with your children, the more realistically you will be able to assess their capacities, and the more aware you will be of their particular talents and sensibilities. You will then be able to provide the stimulation that will be optimal for their development.

Spending more time with your child will enhance his self-esteem. Your time is precious to both of you. Your willingness to give your time to him sends a message: You are important.

The closer the relationship you have with your child, the more likely your child will continue to identify with you. You will, therefore, be in an advantageous position to instill your positive values, and increase the likelihood that they will be accepted.

Don't let yourself off the hook by saying, "I don't have much time with my child, but the time we do have together is *quality time.*" The spontaneous and telltale expressions of your child's inner world will not necessarily occur during the 7:30–8:00 P.M. slot you have allotted to him. It takes time to truly understand your child and the drama of his life. It takes time to resist the temptation to answer his questions with, "Because that's just the way it is," or, "Because I told you so." It takes time and shared experiences to build a bond with your child.

YOU HAVE THE DUTY TO FIND MORE PATIENCE FOR YOUR CHILD.

It is difficult to be tired, stressed-out, angry, or unhappy, and still be a good parent. It is difficult to be an understanding parent when you are always functioning on the edge. For the sake of your children, reduce the stress and unhappiness in your life. Because they are children, they will be frustrating, demanding, unreasonable, whiny, rebellious, and clumsy. You must be able to deal with all of that.

YOU HAVE THE DUTY TO LET YOUR CHILD BE HIMSELF.

As parents, we can't help hoping that our children will adopt our values and priorities. (After having children I suddenly became enamored of the idea of arranged marriages. Having lived three times as long as my children, having been married for several decades, wouldn't I have a more astute judgment about the kind of person who would make good "marriage material"?) But we must encourage *their* talents and potential. Keep your fantasies for their future in check. Help them find *their* way.

YOU HAVE A DUTY TO LOVE YOUR CHILD.

Just because you love your child does not mean that he feels loved. You must *demonstrate* your love. Don't talk to your child while your head is buried in the newspaper. "Uh-huh" is an insufficient response to your child's lengthy story about how she had a fight with her best friend, the unfairness of the world, and her subsequent feelings that "Nobody likes me. I hate my life." You must indicate that what is important to her is important to you. You must see the world through your child's eyes so you can appreciate how painful it can be for her, instead of thinking, "Don't be ridiculous. That's silly." Remember, also, to love your child when he disappoints you. Finally, make sure you give your child much more praise than criticism. Let your child know what is right about him.

Loving should be daily. And it should be explicit. I admit it. I used to embarrass my daughter Sarah. When she was younger, every day I asked her the same question, "How much does Daddy love you?" When she was preverbal, I supplied the answer, "A lot," or, "A lot, a lot, a lot, a lot." Later, when she was capable of providing a response, she impishly grinned and shrieked, "A lot!" Then I said, "Is that all?" She picked up her cue and continued, "A lot, a lot, a lot, a lot." Sometimes, when I asked the question, she rolled her eyes back in her head and protested, "Not again, Dad." I clearly exasperated her.

A small price to pay, I figured.

YOU HAVE A DUTY TO DISCIPLINE WITH LOVE (AND FAIRNESS).

I remember one father who proudly boasted how "responsible" and "involved" he was in parenting his troublesome son. "He's got everything he could want. Much, much more than when I was his age. I treat him fairly, but firmly. I let him know there are ground rules. No TV during the week, one hour on the weekend. I don't allow any back talk. I let him know who's boss. . . . I don't know what his problem is." The limit-setting is fine, but where is the love? I thought.

Yet love is not enough. Children crave guidelines. They will learn how to control themselves from you, and your effectiveness in teaching discipline will greatly determine your child's future success in imposing mechanisms of self-regulation. Will your son be overly critical of himself, unforgiving, unable to feel comfortable with any gratification? Or will he be excessively self-indulgent to the point of self-destruction? Will he be able to find a middle ground that will provide a balanced sense of responsibility *and* self-satisfaction?

Will your daughter be able to tolerate frustration? Will she accept the fact that she cannot always have what her heart desires, or will she feel forever deprived and resentful? Will she concede that others have urgent needs as well, needs that may not coincide with her own but that, nevertheless, must be respected? In other words, will she be able to relate to others in a loving, unselfish manner? Or will she fervently believe she deserves whatever she wants and, therefore, be unable to have a mature relationship?

Encourage progress. Encourage *effort*. Some of the parents of my children's friends promise their sons and daughters amounts of money if they attain certain grades. But when we give our children a reward for getting A's in school or making the all-star team, we communicate an unhealthy message: You are as good as what you achieve. And if our children believe an A or the all-star team is beyond their grasp, they will simply give up. Encourage effort. Teach your children that the end product is less important than the process of trying their best.

In order to discipline appropriately and effectively, it is critical that you have realistic expectations. What should you reasonably expect from your ten-year-old daughter as opposed to your three-year-old daughter? What should you reasonably expect of your nine-year-old daughter as opposed to your eight-year-old son? What should you reasonably expect of your child who was born with a "difficult" temperament as opposed to your child who always seems to have a smile on her face?

When your toddler uses your living room couch as a coloring book, you must control your disgust, your anger, and your urge to lash out. You take away the crayons and clearly state that it is not okay to color on furniture. Nothing more. If your child is acting in an age-appropriate manner, it is you who must modify the unrealistic expectations that generate your displeasure and exasperation.

YOU HAVE A DUTY TO TREAT YOUR CHILDREN AS CHILDREN.

I frequently hear a parent comment about the "wisdom of children." Children are not wise. They are innocent, and they are outspoken. But they are not wise. They need your guidance.

Children are also not adults, and we must adjust our expectations accordingly. A father once related to me what a fiasco it was to drive with his wife and two sons (ages eight and six) from Los Angeles to Lake Tahoe, almost five hundred miles away. "My kids were carrying on in the back practically the whole time. They just couldn't sit still. We bought games for them to play, but they'd go through those in minutes. Then, they'd fight with each other. I kept yelling, 'Sit down and be still!' But it didn't matter. It was a nightmare."

"How many times did you stop along the way?" I asked.

"We stopped once for gas," he said. "It's a long drive. I just wanted to get there." One stop? Adults may sit still in a car for nine hours, but children won't. Be realistic. Don't expect children to act like adults.

One of our obligations to our children is to understand their emotional needs and their emotional limits. For example, some mental health professionals encourage parents who are divorcing to tell their children about their own feelings (anger, frustration, sadness, fear) and difficulties concerning their decision. I disagree. At this point in time, children's psychological resources will be maximally strained. Children must not be made to feel more anxious or compelled to take care of their parents. On the contrary, they already feel as though their worlds are falling apart and are entitled to whatever steadying influence you can provide. They need to know that you are still strong and will continue to offer the love and security they desperately require.

On a recent rafting trip with my family, the boat hit a rock and I fell out into the river. The raft continued downstream with my terrified children and wife. Looking back, they saw me go under the water and struggle in the swift current. My younger children, in particular, thought I was dying. When I finally caught up with my family, Sarah and Nathan were crying and shaking with fear. "I'm fine," I reassured them. "I just fell out of the boat, a lot of people do. You know Dad's a good swimmer. I just got a little wet. Listen to me, kids. Dad's strong. I will not drown. Nothing bad like that will *ever* happen to me." This was not the time to launch into a lecture about the perils of the river and the need to be careful. Nor was this an opportunity to disclose how frightened I really was when I had difficulty rising to the surface of the water. This was a moment to focus on my children and their need to be reassured about their father's invincibility.

The parent-child relationship is not merely about honesty. It is foremost about providing our children with a sense of safety and security. Parents do not have the luxury of simply being themselves in front of their children, of letting it all hang out. Your children need to believe in your strength, your constancy, your judgment, and your love.

FOR THE SAKE OF YOUR CHILDREN, YOU HAVE A DUTY TO LOVE YOUR SPOUSE MORE.

Men occupy more positions of recognized status and power than do women. They usually make more money than women, and money is, perhaps, our preeminent symbol of achievement and worth. One result of this state of affairs is that, deep down, the husband tends to believe that his sphere, his work, is more important and more valuable than the one occupied by his wife, who is the mother of his children. This is true even if the wife has a job outside of the home because (1) she is probably earning less than her husband, and (2) she is still expected by her husband to fulfill the bulk of parental responsibilities.

It is ironic; what could be a more "powerful" role than that of the mothers who nurture and shape our children, the future of our society? But just as men do not receive many nods of approbation for being good fathers, women do not receive social recognition for being good mothers. We simply presume that women will be caring, nurturing, competent mothers to their children. We do not reward or acknowledge them for that.

Ask the typical father what is most important to him, and he will answer, "My children." And yet, he does not value his wife's role and her attendant activities involved in nurturing his children as much as he should.

He is pleased that his daughter takes ballet lessons. She has become more graceful, more dexterous, and more beautiful. Who drives her to those lessons? Who bought her those ballet shoes? Who combed her hair in a way that makes her eyes seem to sparkle? He is thrilled about his son doing so well on his Little League baseball team. His son has become more self-confident, more popular with his peers, and more enthusiastic about his life. Who makes sure that his son arrives on time to his practices? Who takes his son's teammates out for ice cream after the practice? Who keeps his son's uniform clean so that he looks like a smaller version of a major league athlete?

Your wife is the keeper of the thing that is most important to you in the entire world. Let her know how much you love her because of how well she cares for your children. Tell her, and then give her a big hug (in front of the kids is best). Do it today.

I do not mean to imply that loving your spouse more is a husband-to-wife, one-way street. But because the traditional husband's efforts often provide more tangible benefits, he is more likely to receive recognition than his wife. Moreover, wives already tend to be more nurturing than their husbands. The fact remains, however, that we all want to feel appreciated and cared about. Let your husband know you do.

When you love your husband more, he will want to be more involved in his family. He knows how much you love your children, and he will, therefore, want to love them as further demonstration of his love for you. Conversely, when a husband feels deprived in a marriage, he is more likely to withdraw from family involvement. An unhappy husband has less patience, less compassion, and less joy to bring to his children. Encourage your husband to be a more involved father, not simply by words, but by your love.

FOR THE SAKE OF YOUR CHILDREN, YOU HAVE A DUTY TO MAKE YOUR MARRIAGE WORK.

During a survey of young people that I conducted many years ago, it became apparent to me that many of them will walk down the aisle on their wedding day thinking, "I wonder how long this will last?" High divorce rates have buried the assumption of "forever after." Because divorce is so commonplace and socially acceptable, we have lost some of our motivations to work on the marriage. ("Work on the marriage!?" one man exclaimed. "I work hard all day. I don't want to work when I come home, too.") We don't stick around long enough to discover that there is an ebb and flow to marriage, that fifty-year relationships may have prolonged periods of ups and downs. Moreover, we live in a world that advises us, If it doesn't feel good, don't do it.

Several years ago, I was watching a television program in which single men and women were interviewed about what they look for in the opposite sex. The most common response was some variation of, "We've got to be able to have fun together." The second most common response was more specific: "There's got to be a physical chemistry."

A young couple came to see me because they weren't sure about whether they should take the next step to marriage. They were both in their early twenties and had been sweethearts since high school. "We really get along. We enjoy doing the same things. We laugh a lot together. And the sex is great," Marty offered.

"We have the same values. We are both into family. And we never fight," Susan added.

"You *never* fight?" I inquired.

"Never." Susan and Marty grinned.

"Then you shouldn't get married yet," I provocatively stated.

Marriage is not simply about having fun together (although that's important). It's not about great sex. (Sex can't stay *great* for fifty years.) Having similar values, although vital, is an insufficient guarantor of marriage as well. Husband and wife must be able to satisfactorily resolve conflict, because conflict is inevitable. They must be able to discuss and negotiate their different desires, instead of becoming defensive or withdrawn. They must be able to take and give.

Husbands and wives do not come to my office after experiencing difficulties for a week or for a month. By the time they make an appointment with me, they have usually endured years of frustration, broken promises ("I'll try harder"), and dashed fantasies. They feel helpless and hopeless.

Indeed, some of those marriages are hopeless. But I have also been fortunate enough to see many of those crumbling relationships rejuvenate themselves. People fall into patterns of criticism, counterattack, and withdrawal. They become too angry to act generously, and too bitter to forgive. But this mutually destructive cycle can also be reversed when husband and wife can be brought back in touch with their deep caring for one another, and taught how to talk again without becoming defensive and critical.

If you and your spouse feel stuck in patterns of attack and counterattack, or mutual withdrawal, you owe it to yourselves and your children to seek professional help. Especially when children are part of the picture, you must explore every avenue in trying to keep your family intact.

When couples divorce, fathers often become more distant from their sons and daughters. Your children need two parents. They deserve two parents.

Your Duty to the Stranger

WE HAVE DUTIES TO THOSE EMOTIONALLY CLOSEST TO US AND THOSE more removed. But more than ever, we fear the stranger. We used to fear difference—someone who did not dress the way we do, someone whose skin was a color other than ours, someone whose customs appeared odd, or someone who spoke a foreign language. Now, we fear anyone whom we do not know.

A stranger knocks on your door and pleads, "Can you help me? I was in a car accident down the street and my child is hurt." Would you hesitate? Would you ultimately go with him if it were daytime? What if he knocked on your door in the afternoon and asked to use your telephone? What if it were a woman?

How many times have you passed a disabled vehicle on the side of the road and not even thought of stopping to offer assistance? If your car broke down and a stranger approached to offer aid, would you feel grateful or wary? (I recently attended traffic school for having "rolled through" a stop sign. The instructor advised: "If your car is disabled and someone approaches to offer help, don't lower your window. Simply tell him, 'Thanks, I've already called for help.'")

Even superficial familiarity seems to lessen our apprehension about the stranger. Studies consistently demonstrate that when a "victim" strikes up a brief, trivial conversation with a subject before pretending to have a seizure, the subject is more than twice as likely to offer assistance than when the victim and subject are complete strangers. Just slight acquaintance can breed compassion and a sense of responsibility.

We too easily turn away from strangers in need and, subsequently, justify our indifference. A homeless person approaches on the street and asks for a quarter. You say to yourself, "He'll only spend it on alcohol," and continue on. Perhaps next time you could think, What would help him? Your response might then be, "I won't give you a quarter, but I will buy you a sandwich." We have all heard stories about the profound gratitude of an individual who was given a job, an opportunity for physical sustenance that also allowed him to maintain his dignity.

We feel a natural desire to help our family and friends. When it comes to the stranger, however, we must combat our fear and indifference. Helping the stranger must, therefore, emanate from a commitment to fulfill a higher obligation, an obligation to help the needy, whoever he may be. Our humanity is tested not when we assist those close to us, but when we extend ourselves to the stranger, simply because it's the right thing to do.

Being Moral and Being Selfish Are Compatible

THE CONTEST BETWEEN SELF-INTEREST AND SELF-SACRIFICE IS A never-ending one. Acting out of a firm sense of duty keeps us from being swayed by transitory feelings. But let us be clear. Putting another first does not divert us from the path of self-actualization (except when we *always* put others first). On the contrary. When we give freely, we reinforce our sense of security and announce a strength of character. We look at our behavior and know that it is a reflection of the good that lies within.

When we act generously, we diminish our anxieties. We realize that we have more than we feared we had. When we act considerately, we learn that we don't always have to be preoccupied with ourselves in order to thrive.

During a debate on the inherent nature of man, I once heard a cynic declare, "Good people are people who enjoy doing good things. So, they are still acting selfishly." But the enjoyment I feel from doing good does not simply derive from the act itself. It springs from seeing the effect my behavior has on you. Pleasure envelops me because my behavior affirms my reassuring connection to you. My benevolent acts declare, I am in this with you, you are in this with me. And that is a comfort.

Life is too difficult to be in it alone.

A couple of challenges:

In the coming week, go to a place that voluntarily cares for the needy (such as a homeless shelter, a soup kitchen, the Salvation Army) and ask, "What can I do to help?"

In your dealings with strangers during the coming week, treat them as though they were distant cousins.

CHAPTER SIX

Dignity

WE HAVE A DUTY TO HELP PEOPLE FEEL good about themselves.

The black Episcopal archbishop, Desmond Tutu, won the Nobel prize for his efforts in opposing the oppressive white regime of South Africa. When asked about the most formative experiences of his life, he replied, "One incident comes to mind immediately. When I was a young child, I saw a white man tip his hat to a black woman. Please understand that such a gesture was completely unheard of in my country. The white man was an Episcopal bishop and the black woman was my mother."

We hunger for dignity. When it is denied us, we wilt from the lack of nourishment to our soul. Or we simmer with rage at such a basic affront to our humanity. One of the most profound influences you can have on me is to foster or stifle my self-respect.

In his *Critique of Practical Reason*, Immanuel Kant wrote of the obligation always to treat a person as an end and not a means. Almost two hundred years later, Lawrence Kohlberg urged that to act justly, with respect for the individual, is to "act so as to treat each person as an end, as having unconditional value, rather than a means."

To put it in a slightly different way, we must always relate to another's humanness, rather than his function. Instead of simply asking, "What can you do for me?" I must first acknowledge that you are a person with the same needs and sensibilities as I have. The chambermaid is not merely an individual who cleans my hotel room. The gas attendant is not merely someone who fills my car with gas. The waiter is not merely a figure who delivers my food. These are all people with feelings, with burdens.

When I treat you as an object, as a means to an end, I deny your worthiness. My behavior says, You are lower than I am, you are less deserving than me. My actions declare, I am more important than you.

We are most likely to steal another's dignity in a situation where there is a perceived social inequality, for example, between the chambermaid and the hotel guest. But also among peers, in a networking breakfast, for instance, there is danger inherent in this utilitarian outlook. For, even when there is little disguise of my intention (we are all here to advance our business fortunes), networking implies that treating one another as functions, as means to an end, is completely acceptable. The networking world is one where the *only* way you consider me is to assess whether I can be of any value to your endeavor. Can we confidently assume that this kind of interaction, with its lack of human regard, can so easily be compartmentalized that it does not spill over to the rest of our life? I think not.

Your acquaintance, Bob, urges you to call Howard. "He's a very successful guy. You should invite him to lunch. You never know when you might be able to do some business together." So, you call Howard. "Bob told me you're a terrific guy. He thought it would be a good idea for us to meet one another. Let me buy you lunch sometime next week."

We act more generously to those who are "making it." Ironically, we are the most giving of ourselves to those who are highly success-ful, those who probably need our generosity less than those who are struggling to get by. We treat the gas attendant and the waiter with indifference, because they provide us with little potential oppor-tunity.

Treat me as you would like to be treated. Help me feel good about myself. When I feel good about myself, I will be kinder to you and to everyone around us.

Aren't I Important Enough?

WE ARE EXTREMELY SENSITIVE TO THE SLIGHTS OF OTHERS BECAUSE we so crave dignity. A few months ago, I twice called an acquain-tance, a highly regarded writer and lecturer, and left messages at both of his telephone numbers. He is someone I have never tele-phoned, but we have known each other for over twenty years. Our paths periodically crossed at public forums and at the homes of common friends, where we would engage in warm and personal conversation. I had always liked him. He is intelligent, witty, erudite, and serious-minded. I had believed there was a recognition of mu-tual respect and a certain degree of genuine caring. My unprece-dented calls were due to a matter of some urgency that I wanted to discuss with him.

He never responded. But we ran into one another again a few weeks later. "I know you've been trying to get ahold of me. I got your mes-sages, but I've just been so busy," he mumbled. That was it. No apol-ogy. No inquiry to say, Why were you calling? (Keep in mind that, in twenty years of acquaintanceship, I had never telephoned him. Wouldn't my call imply, therefore, some import?) No need to treat me as a person, as an equal. No need to consider what prompted me. All that kept going through my mind while we exchanged pleasantries was, "He didn't even care to know why I was calling."

It is when I am most needy that I will feel your slight most acutely. I reach out, only to be met with your disinterest. I am unworthy of your attention, I feel.

Everyday dishonesties often highlight issues of inferiority and superiority. They "put you in your place."

"Hello, I'd like to speak to Mr. Thompson."

"He's on the phone, may I tell him who is calling?"

"Gary Reed."

A few seconds of silence as the assistant speaks with her boss.

"I'm sorry, he's not available and will have to get back to you."

In other words, you were not important enough for Mr. Thompson to have taken your call. But you squelch your resentment at the rudeness of it all and politely comply with the assistant's request for your telephone number so that "Mr. Thompson can return your call." And he never does.

If you are truly overwhelmed, you have a right to husband your time. But if that is the case, tell your assistant in advance, "I'm busy. Hold all calls," or "Hold all calls except for Mr. Smith and Ms. Jones." Spare me the rejection of "I'll see if Mr. Thompson is available." And unless I have been an obnoxious bother in the past, give me the courtesy of picking up the telephone when your assistant tells you of my request.

The philosopher Paul Tillich advised: "The first duty of love is to listen."

In *The Ten Challenges*, psychologist Leonard Felder notes another common slight that undermines our dignity:

Interrupting someone in conversation is another type of stealing of self-worth. Especially if the person speaking needs to be heard and understood, the abruptness of a sudden interruption or a sarcastic and demeaning "Get to the point already!" can be quite jarring. In some families, one person repeatedly cuts off other family members. In some relationships, the inability or unwillingness of one partner to listen patiently to the other can be the cause of numerous fights or even a breakup. The phrase commonly used for this habit of cutting people off in conversation is "stealing the floor." There's no prison sentence or monetary fine for it, but from a spiritual point of view it's thievery nonetheless.

Everyone wants to feel that he is important enough to consider.

Leave Your Pity at the Door

WHEN I AM TROUBLED, I PARTICULARLY WANT YOU TO LISTEN. I WANT your compassion. But I would recoil from your pity. Lawrence Hinman, a professor of philosophy at the University of California at San Diego, critically distinguishes between the effects of pity and compassion.

When I am the object of your pity, I see you looking down on me.

When I am the object of your pity, I can tell that you see me as somehow responsible for my plight.

When I am the object of your pity, I know you are not moved to share my pain.

When I am the object of your pity, I believe you don't truly understand me.

When I am the object of your pity, I question if you are sincerely interested in me, or view me as a vessel through which you can demonstrate your social conscience.

When I am the object of your pity, I know you are separating yourself from me.

When you express genuine compassion, you reach out and involve yourself in my suffering. When you express genuine compassion, you do not assume I am to be blamed. When you express genuine compassion, you understand me. When you express genuine compassion, you tell me I am your equal.

Flattery

WHENEVER YOU RECOGNIZE ME, I WANT IT TO BE A GENUINE ACK-knowledgment of my humanity. So, as seductive as it might be, I don't want your flattery. While we are obliged to encourage another's self-worth, we should refrain from contrived compliments.

I know someone who greets nearly every woman or man she knows with, "You look great!" If confronted with her obvious pattern of flattery, she would probably retort: "I'm just making people feel good. What's so bad about that?" But here we have a wonderful example of seemingly benign behavior having potentially deleterious consequences. Three of those consequences come to mind: (1) When you are dishonest with others, you will further anticipate their dishonesty in return. ("That's the way the game works.") Anticipating dishonesty leads to cynicism. Indeed, my acquaintance is an extremely mistrustful individual. (2) Flattery is often transparent. The one you are flattering will likely perceive you to be a liar, thereby increasing his cynicism as well. (3) If the individual had accepted the compliment at face value, he will be hurt and disappointed when he hears my acquaintance voice the same insincere sentiments to all other comers.

(Anticipating the moral quandaries in Section Two, let me offer one that a friend recently raised: You are hosting a fund-raising event for a charity. What if you spotted a rich man who had not, as yet, made a commitment, and whom you knew was easily swayed by flattery. Would it be okay to stroke his ego for a good cause? What do you do when issues of disingenuousness, using a person as a means to an end, and actions for a good cause collide?)

Unhelpful Criticism

WE SHOULDN'T UNNECESSARILY FLATTER, BUT WE MUST ENCOURAGE. Unfortunately, we tend only to appreciate results as opposed to effort. And many of us criticize much more than we praise, thereby dampening enthusiasm and squelching confidence. One father I counseled about his nine-year-old son, Jonathan, exclaimed, "He never does *anything* right!" Anything? Impossible.

Adults do it to adults as well. Why do many of us so focus on another's missteps or failures? Oftentimes, it is because you want to prove that you are smarter than me, that you are *better* than me. Or, you want to prove that you were right and that I was wrong. Or, you want to demonstrate how much more integrity you have than I do.

There is another common reason some of us are very critical and impatient. Unhappy people vent their frustrations and resentments at handy targets. Criticism often serves as a ready-made vehicle for the expression of your anger and your sense that the world has dealt you an unfair hand. Furthermore, when you criticize, you don't have to acknowledge your reservoir of anger. You can cloak your comments in noble robes. "I was only trying to help."

We need guidance. We need feedback designed to keep us moving in a healthy, productive direction. I don't want you simply to be my cheerleader. I need you to tell me when I am being unreasonable and unrealistic.

There is one kind of criticism, however, whose effect is solely destructive. It is when you find fault with something I can do nothing about. There is no point in ever allowing your dark-haired, brown-eyed spouse to know that you prefer blond hair and blue eyes. It is cruel to comment to your slim wife that you find large breasts a real turn-on. It is insensitive to go on and on about how articulate and charismatic you find Arthur to be, when your husband, Randy, is an unassuming man of few words.

Criticism, delivered properly, can be helpful when change is within our grasp. Asking me to change what is already etched in stone will only cause me to feel unworthy and resentful.

One change, however, requires that we simply shift some of our energies and become aware of somewhat different priorities. We teach our children to respect the environment and set aside days for recycling in order to demonstrate that respect. Adults dutifully separate their garbage, putting aside paper, aluminum, glass, and plastic products so they can have another life. I propose a nationally recognized day each year on which we are especially mindful of treating others with dignity—when we relate to others as humans not objects, as equals not inferiors, as encouragers not critics, as people with the same desires for recognition.

Everyone Judges

EVERYONE HAS AN OPINION. I AM ALWAYS AMAZED WHEN I SEE THE results of questions asked in national polls: Should the United States send the military to intervene in Bosnia? Should Congress pass NAFTA? Do you favor the inclusion of former Communist states in NATO? What amazes me are the number of individuals who voice an opinion one way or another, while possessing so little knowledge of the complex issues involved.

We feel compelled to sort out right and wrong, safe and dangerous. The philosopher John Dewey wrote that "insecurity generates the quest for certainty." For hundreds of thousands of years, we have needed to quickly assess, Is he friend or is he foe? That penchant for instant and sure judgment has remained with us today.

We judge for reasons other than a desire for safety, as well. We judge another's physical appearance ("I'm so much thinner than her"), income ("He's not very successful"), dress ("How could she wear that?!"), children ("They were so poorly behaved"), intelligence

("He's not a rocket scientist"), sense of humor ("He has none"), and morality ("How could he do that?!") in order to distance ourselves from the fear of being the same. I am definitely not like him, we declare. We judge others harshly in order to obliterate our insecurities. Truly confident people are not critical people. They don't need to be.

We all judge. But do we have a right to judge? There are many who believe that we must refrain. Who are you to judge me? you insist. And, besides, if that's what I feel, who are you to tell me otherwise? My feelings, my opinions, are just as valid as yours. We are all equal, you sincerely assert.

The stance of "We shouldn't judge others" is not simply motivated by your humanistic impulses, however. Two other self-serving motives come to mind: (1) If you judge me, I might turn around and find fault with you, and (2) If you advocate a position of, "He was driven to do that because of his anger (or his fear, or his insecurities), and therefore we should not condemn him," you have provided a ready excuse for your own past, present, or future moral failures.

Do we have the right to judge another's behavior, given that we have all acted immorally at one time or another? In *Why Good People Do Bad Things*, Bruce Hamstra, a counseling psychologist, provides a reply.

Let's be honest about this: Although we may couch our observations in other terms, we make judgments about people and their activities all the time. *If we jump to conclusions based on prejudice, bias, and lack of information, we are in fact being judgmental in the worst sense of the word.* Nevertheless, we are living in a world that requires us to make judgments about our own and other people's *deeds.* To do so is quite dangerous, yet the alternatives may be far worse. Lines must be drawn, judgments must be reached.

Tolerance for others does not necessitate a withholding of judgment. You may be tolerant and choose not to interfere with what I am doing. However, you don't have to approve of it by your silence. You can tell me you think I am wrong. But be careful. Make sure you apply the same standards to yourself as you demand of me, and not just in areas of your "convenience zone." "I am considerate of my neighbor, and you should be, too," you admonish. But what about that extramarital affair you are having, or your lack of charity?

Judgment need not imply rejection or ostracism. There is an important distinction between judging (and implicitly rejecting) a *person*, and judging his *actions*. When you judge my actions, you remind me and you of what's right. When you judge my actions, you prod me to make amends, and you help guide me in future decisions.

Yes, I can judge your *behavior*, and you can judge mine. But since all of us have flaws, wouldn't you want me to refrain from rejecting you because of your stubbornness, your stinginess, your compulsivity, your narcissism, your promiscuity, your competitiveness, or your materialistic side? Yet we turn our nose up at someone who qualifies for any of these. (In reality, none of us would have any friends if we only associated with people who were devoid of imperfections. My friend Arnie is stubborn, controlling, and can have a bad temper. But he is also generous, bright, and has many of the same cultural passions as I do. My friend Joan can be very competitive. But she is also supportive, reliable, and very compassionate. We have to ignore and/or accept certain qualities if we are to have *any* close relationships.)

We try to hide our deficiencies from public view. If others really knew us, they would know we are somewhat less than what meets the eye. Does that mean we are bad people? No. Does that mean we have fears and insecurities that drive us to be less than we can be? Of course.

We should all act from our higher self, we should all aim for a moral bull's-eye. But let us stop giving others a harder time than we give ourselves. Let us stop simplifying others while retaining a self-image of proud complexity. (Imagine how offended you would be if I said, "You know, you're a rather simple person.") Let us stop assuming others are less sensitive than we are. But let us hold others responsible when they do what is wrong.

Gossip

I AM SURE THAT YOU HAVE KNOWN THE PAIN AND *HELPLESSNESS* OF finding out that a friend, a colleague, or a neighbor has spread private and embarrassing information about you, *whether it was false or true.* Few things can make us feel so naked or so undignified as gossip.

In the Introduction, I mentioned how quickly we evaluate others and how difficult it is for that impression to be modified. In just moments, you decide what kind of person I am, and whether you like me or not. To paraphrase Leonard Felder, it might take only five seconds for someone to spread some dirt about me, and then it might take me five months, five years, or the rest of my life to regain the respect and trust I have lost in your eyes.

Despite its potentially devastating effects, most of us partake of gossip. Robin Dunbar, a professor of psychology at the University of Liverpool, has studied the phenomenon, and reported his conclusions in *Grooming, Gossip, and the Evolution of Language*, published in 1997. Professor Dunbar's systematic eavesdropping has found that people devote about two-thirds of any conversation to gossip. Furthermore, contrary to popular wisdom, he found no significant differences between men and women, or clerks and corporate executives. Who is sleeping with whom, and do the spouses know? Who was observed hitting her child? Who appears well-off, but doesn't have a cent in the bank? Who has a drug habit? Clearly, people enjoy talking about other people.

Think about this for a moment: When you have heard talk about others, what percentage of the time was spent damning him, and what percentage of the time was spent praising him? How often does someone relate, "Did you hear how Harry spent an entire day helping his neighbor fix a leaky roof?" or "Did you know that Mary visited her sick friend every day she was in the hospital?" or "Isn't it incredible how Roger volunteered to serve on another school committee?"

No, we don't gossip about people's noble efforts or shining qualities, even though we *should* publicize them. In fact, we tend to ignore them.

Why?

We gossip because we want to feel morally superior. Evidence for this desire is how easily we accept the information as true and complete, regardless of the source. We don't consider how well the source knows the victim, how biased the source might be toward the victim, how much of the context of the behavior the source is considering, or even if the source's information is firsthand. We certainly don't think of the victim, "I wonder what made him do that?"

We gossip to distance ourself from "that kind of behavior," to indicate we would never stoop so low. "Can you believe what Chet and Roberta did?!" we rhetorically ask in mock horror.

We gossip out of boredom. We fill our own life with the excitement of others' escapades. At least someone is eating of the forbidden fruit.

Sometimes, we gossip in order to exact revenge. It is not only that I want to hurt Sally by spreading unflattering pictures of her. I want to enlist you in my vindictive cause by planting seeds of my resentment toward Sally in you. I want you on my side in this vendetta. If you also come to see Sally in the damning light I bathe her in, my attitude and anger will feel even more righteous.

A final reason we gossip may not be so readily apparent. We talk about others as a way to avoid talking about ourselves. Our relationship seems close and personal, but you and I talk about *other* persons. We are discussing sensitive issues—sexual escapades, failings, weaknesses—but not our own. And all the time we are doing this, we imply, "But I'm okay. I would never do that."

In *Words That Hurt, Words That Heal,* Joseph Telushkin points out that even when the information is true, we should refrain from passing it on.

The *fairness* of disseminating negative information is a particularly important but frequently overlooked criterion by people who gossip. I often ask lecture audiences: "How many of you can think of at least one episode in your life that would cause you great embarrassment were it to become known to everyone else here?"

Usually, almost every hand goes up except those who have poor memories, or who have led exceptionally boring lives, or are lying. I suspect that most people who raise their hands are not concealing a history of armed robbery. Nevertheless, were a particularly embarrassing episode known to the public, it might disproportionately influence others' impressions of that person. Because such information would probably be unusual, it might even become the primary association other people have with the person, which of course is the very reason he or she wants it kept private. Thus, although such information is true, disseminating it would be unfair.

We hunger for more control over our life. Gossip, by its very nature, then, feeds our insecurities. True or untrue, gossip is out there, wending its way along an unpredictable path.

A well-known Hasidic story emphasizes the brutality of gossip and its power to leave lifelong wounds. In this tale, a student has been spreading hurtful rumors about his teacher. At one point, however, he experiences remorse and approaches his teacher to ask for forgiveness.

The teacher suggests, "If you want to make amends for what you've done, I recommend taking several feather pillows, cutting them open, and letting the wind disperse the feathers."

The student does as he was told and returns to the teacher, who says calmly, "Now, there's one more step. Go out and gather up all the feathers."

The student replies, "But how can I do that? It's impossible. The winds have scattered them in every direction."

The teacher explains, "Now you're beginning to learn about the power of words. Once you have started or repeated a hurtful rumor and it spreads in all directions, it is very difficult to try to undo all the damage."

Apologizing

IN A WAY, IT SEEMS SO OBVIOUS. IF YOU DO SOMETHING HURTFUL TO me, you must acknowledge it. So, why do you have such difficulty saying, "I was wrong?"

If you have hurt me, you are reluctant to say you were wrong because you fear that your admission will imply that you are a bad person. That is why, even when you do say "I was wrong," or "I'm sorry for what I did to you," you immediately add your justifications: "I was having a bad day," or "I've been overly sensitive lately," or "I just didn't realize that . . ." We find reasons that are temporary, reasons that affirm, I am still a basically good individual.

I see this difficulty in purely admitting, "I was wrong," nearly every day in my office when couples attempt to reconcile after a bitter argument or serious breach of the relationship.

"I shouldn't have said that, but I was just so hurt."

"I didn't mean to have the affair, but I've been so frustrated."

"I probably wouldn't have done that if you hadn't——before."

The husbands and wives do not simply say, "I was wrong." And even when they do get the words out, they refuse to accept responsibility for their actions. "I'm sorry. But, if you hadn't——, I wouldn't have——." The apology is briefly given, and then snatched away.

You can have an incredibly powerful effect on your partner by simply and clearly apologizing. When you say, "I was wrong" (and stop there), her anger will instantly deflate. Days or weeks of cultivated resentment will collapse because all she wanted was an admission of your wrongdoing, an acknowledgment of the pain you have caused her. When you admit your mistake without excusing it, you also communicate, "You are precious to me, and I shouldn't treat you inconsiderately." Period.

Whether it be with a lover or an acquaintance, many of us experience the acknowledgment of wrongdoing as a defeat. If you apologize, I am now one up in our moral competition. You now have to provide some additional proof in the future that you are really okay, that I can trust you. You feel more vulnerable, fearing that I may hold your misstep over you. I might even use it as an excuse to betray you. Moreover, your acceptance of responsibility for your misconduct in this instance might affect your wider reputation, as well. Your entire character may now come under closer scrutiny.

Nevertheless, when you have hurt me, intentionally or otherwise, you owe me. You owe me a clear recognition of that hurt, and a sincere desire to make amends.

When you apologize, you need to offer more than regret. Ideally, apology should involve a three-step process. The first step is the acknowledgment of *exactly* what you have done that was wrong. So, instead of, "I know that what I did yesterday was wrong," try, "I know that when I lied to you about where I went yesterday afternoon, I was wrong." The second step is recognizing the effect of your behavior. "I know that when I lied to you it made you feel betrayed by me." And the third step is to ask what you can do to make up for your mistake. "What can I do to restore your trust in me?"

Unfortunately, many of us carry grudges and resentments far too long. It is never too late, therefore, to apologize. You can remove the burden of another's disappointment, and restore some of his confidence in people. He needs to know that you feel remorse for your behavior, so that the world will not seem like such an insensitive, brutal arena. When you think about it, that's a wonderful offering of peace.

Forgiving

THERE IS A VERY MOVING TRADITION THAT MANY JEWS ENGAGE IN BEfore their New Year. They call those who are dear to them and plead, "I hope you will forgive me if I hurt you in any way this past year." The tradition emphasizes that how I treat my fellow man is even more important than how I relate to God.

It is critical to note that I do not necessarily ask forgiveness for any specific action. Indeed, there may not be anything I have done that I believe hurt the other person. So, why do I make the request?

Three reasons come to mind: (1) My request affirms that I have an obligation to be sensitive to you. (2) By asking for your forgiveness, I declare your worth. I make clear that you are important enough to care about, that I wish to preserve our relationship. When my acquaintance failed to apologize for not returning my phone calls, it hurt because I assumed that I wasn't important enough for him to be concerned about. Apologies can have such a powerful effect because *we want our worth acknowledged.* (3) I don't always know when I have hurt you, so I cover myself in case I have.

The New Year custom I described is not just about apology. It also calls for the other person's forgiveness. All of us struggle with emotional baggage—old hurts, resentments, and insecurities that cause us to act imperfectly. When you forgive me, you acknowledge that we are all fallible, that we all have weaknesses.

Forgiveness implies, I believe you can be better, and I want to give you that opportunity. Forgiveness does not suggest excuse. In fact, the philosopher and theologian Moses Maimonides took the extreme position that you should forgive only after I have faced a similar situation in the future and acted correctly.

It is sometimes so difficult for us to forgive, for us to give up our hurt and righteous indignation. But wouldn't you want to be forgiven for your missteps? When you are forgiven, you are not only unburdened of guilt, but you are also relieved of the pressure to be perfect. When I forgive you, I accept you.

You cannot change what has happened in the past. I can't take back what I intentionally or unintentionally did to you. But you *can* change how you will continue to allow my behavior to affect you.

Sometimes, you just feel too hurt to be able to forgive, to be able to wipe the slate clean. But the weight of your anger and hatred is ultimately only self-destructive. Angry people remain unhappy people. Anger holds you back. It prevents you from continuing freely with your life. Scholem Asch begins his novel *The Nazarene*: "Not the power to remember, but its very opposite, the power to forget, is a necessary condition of our existence."

When we are hurt by another, we are also shaken by a glimpse at our powerlessness, our lack of control over what the world can do to us. Harold Kushner understands our need to counteract this impotence.

The embarrassing secret is that many of us are reluctant to forgive. We nurture grievances because that makes us feel morally superior. Withholding forgiveness gives us a sense of power, often power over someone who otherwise leaves us feeling powerless. The only power we have over them is the power to remain angry at them.

When I retain my anger toward you, I maintain an illusion that I am actually punishing you.

But anger causes us to withdraw, when what we need most are caring connections to others. To forgive is to allow the relationship to move forward, uncontaminated by past mistakes and old hurts. When you truly forgive, you remove the toxin of bitterness from your system and replace it with the elixir of hope.

Asking for Help

IT IS DIFFICULT FOR MANY OF US, ESPECIALLY MEN, TO ASK FOR HELP. In the minds of the reluctant, to ask for help implies inadequacy and defeat. We feel more *publicly* vulnerable. The secret is out: I can't take care of myself. I need you because you are stronger (or wiser, or more competent) than I am. With all of these potential implications, no wonder I may feel anxious when I admit that I need some assistance.

An Indian proverb states: "Why do you hate me—I never even helped you."

I don't want to feel that I am less than you, particularly if we are supposed to be equals. The more you resemble me, the greater will be my reluctance to ask for your aid. If you are higher in status or position, I will feel more comfortable approaching you for help. Acknowledging your greater power or expertise would only be admitting the self-evident. But if we are "on the same level," I leave myself vulnerable to your thinking that I am not really your peer. I might even turn on myself and worry that I am not as good, or as smart, or as competent as you.

Other factors influence our readiness to ask for help, as well.

Women seek more help than men. Despite other changes in cultural perceptions, women are still not expected to be as competent as men in many traditionally male bastions—repairs, finance, or dealing with emergencies, to name a few. When a woman asks for help, therefore, she is much less likely to experience her request as evidence of personal inadequacy, with its attendant feelings of enhanced vulnerability.

Those high in socioeconomic status make more requests for help than those low on the status ladder. Those lower on the ladder are less likely to have the confidence (and resulting ability to be assertive) of the more successful. Those higher in status are more likely to feel entitled to assistance than those less well-off. I have noticed how startlingly more confident individuals can become when their fortunes take a dramatic upturn. (Unfortunately, we have all seen how often money is also accompanied by arrogance.)

So many of us find it difficult to ask for help—I didn't even mention the shy, the depressed, the control freaks, those acutely sensitive to rejection, to name a few categories—that it behooves you and me simply to be more sensitive to others' needs. You must *anticipate* how you might be helpful. Particularly when you know someone well, when you are familiar with his ongoing struggles or temporary upheavals, anticipating how you might be helpful is not hard to do.

As an exercise, think about your answers to the following, while remembering that I am someone with physical, emotional, and spiritual sides:

If my spouse of fifty years died, what might I need?
If my child were seriously ill, what might I need?
If my wife suddenly asked for a divorce after twenty years of marriage, what might I need?
If I recently lost my job, what might I need?
If my wife were away on an extended business trip, and I were left with my three children to care for, what might I need?
If I just moved into your neighborhood, what might I need?
If I were scolded earlier this afternoon by our mutual boss, what might I need?

If I were agonizing over a decision regarding two career paths, what might I need?

If it were holiday time and I had no family in this city, what might I need?

The Pitfalls of Advice

ONE FORM OF HELPING IS GIVING ADVICE. WE COULD ALL USE THE well-intentioned, caring wisdom of others. My experience, my outlook is, by definition, singularly limited. I need your different way of looking at things, the knowledge you have gained from your contact with certain kinds of people and situations I have never known. I need your objectivity to counterbalance my irrational impulses born of insecurity and old hurts. I need your clarity when I am confused.

But sometimes your motives for giving advice do not emerge from your higher self. Sometimes you offer advice not simply because you are concerned, but in order to show me how much smarter you are. "I'm surprised you haven't thought about———." Sometimes you use the platform of advice to launch into a criticism of me, to pay me back for some other grievance. "If you only weren't so stubborn all the time, you would have realized that what you should have said was———."

Advice is difficult enough to accept without my having to be wary of your underlying agenda. We instinctively recoil from advice because it reminds us of our old childlike position that we have struggled to overcome. I want to be big and strong and independent. I don't want to have to rely on anyone anymore. I'm an adult. I don't want to be told what I should or shouldn't do.

If I unplug my ears and listen to your advice, I might also hear what, deep down, I don't want to do.

"I know these cigarettes are killing me (cough, cough)," you acknowledge.

149

"If you want to stop, I heard of this patch device that is supposed to be very effective. Try chewing gum. I know someone who found relaxation or visualization exercises to be helpful," your friend replies.

"I enjoy cigarettes. I want to smoke," you're thinking.

"Being with Michael just makes me more and more depressed. The relationship is just not good for me," you admit.

"You've got to get out. Michael's just a mean, insensitive slug. He only cares about himself. The sooner the better. Tell him, 'I just can't take your abuse anymore. I deserve better than you.' " Now your friend is really on a roll. "If he says he needs you, and he promises to change, tell him you've heard that before. Don't give him any opening. Do it tonight. I know you're afraid of being alone. Don't worry, you can stay with me for a while until you get settled."

"But I love Michael. I want it to work," you cry silently.

When am I more likely to accept your advice?

I am more likely to accept your advice if I believe your motives are pure, if I believe your desire is only to help.

I am more likely to accept your advice if I believe you have more expertise with this kind of dilemma than I do.

I am more likely to accept your advice if I am desperate and confused.

I am more likely to accept your advice if I truly want to change my situation.

I am more likely to accept your advice if I have seen you successfully solve a similar problem in your own life.

I am more likely to accept your advice if I think you are a level-headed, clear thinker.

I am more likely to accept your advice if I perceive that my abilities to carry it out are adequate.

I am more likely to accept your advice if I perceive the cost to be minimal. (In this case, you may have to help me understand that I can't really lose much, even though I *feel* like the risk could have devastating results. A good example is when I am involved in an obviously destructive love affair, but am too terrified of being alone to end it.)

I am more likely to accept your advice if I believe you have all the relevant facts so that you can offer informed guidance.

I am more likely to accept your advice if I know you are offering what would be best for who I am, and not the person you assume or want me to be.

I am more likely to accept your advice if it allows me to retain my dignity.

So far, I have described the state of mind that will cause me to be more receptive to your advice. But there are also strategies you can employ that will make your advice more attractive.

Before offering suggestions, help me explore my conflict by asking some guiding questions. "What do you imagine might happen if you——?" "How realistic is your fear of——?" "Have you thought about how he might react if you confronted him about——?" "What would you ideally like from——?"

Find out what stabs I have already made in order to resolve my problem. If you offer a suggestion I have attempted in the past that failed, you will lose credibility as my potential guide. "I didn't need you to suggest that, I already tried it," will be my exasperated thought.

Gather as much information as possible about all relevant elements of my particular dilemma and my more general personality before you offer advice. I will reject your counsel if I believe it is hasty or flawed. I will think, "You don't really understand me or my predicament."

Don't contaminate your advice with criticism, such as "I'll tell you what I think you should do, but I can't believe you've gotten yourself into this mess in the first place," or "If you'd listened to me two years ago, this conversation wouldn't be necessary." When you are being critical, I will get angry and defensive. Right now, I need to know that you are on my side. Even if your advice is superb, I will be less likely to hear or accept it if you poison it with criticism.

"Soften" your advice so that I don't feel threatened, forced, or dumb. Use phrases like "Maybe if you tried . . ." or "Perhaps it might be better . . ." or "Have you considered . . ." or "I don't know if this will work for you, but when I was in a similar situation, I . . ."

Present the upside and downside of all of the options instead of simply urging one course of action. Ultimately, I must feel empowered by making my own decision, albeit a more informed one after our conversation.

Avoid any hint of arrogance when you advise me. When I counsel couples, I sometimes refer to my own marriage in order to offer some normative model. For example, I might say, "I know that when my wife reacts to me in that way, I get defensive."

When using my marriage to illustrate a higher standard to aim for, I am very careful. Forty-two-year-old Connie Daniels had been suffering from a mysterious, undiagnosed infection for months. Her husband of fifteen years, Joe, was losing patience with Connie's irritability, lack of sexual interest, and preoccupation with her illness.

"I wish he could be more supportive while I'm having such a hard time," Connie complained. "Instead, he's just angry with me all the time because I'm not there for him. *I'm in pain.* Why can't he understand that?"

"Doc, it's been *months*," Joe countered. "How long can she just expect me to give? Isn't marriage about give *and* take?"

In responding, I wanted to impart a basic principle of marriage. "Please don't misunderstand me. I don't mean to imply that my marriage is perfect, but we are aware that there are going to be prolonged periods when one of us is going to be doing most of the giving."

When I give direct advice about how my patients can improve their relationship, I might preface my remarks with, "I certainly don't always follow my own advice, but I do know what works," or "From personal experience, I know that this is easier said than done, but it's important that you——."

Whether it be asking for help, apologizing, seeking advice, expecting common courtesy, or engaging in judgments of one another, our self-respect is always on the line. We can help others retain their dignity. We can make them feel that they are as good, as worthy, as anyone else. We can reassure them that we are in this *together*.

At a school in the Gisenyi prefecture of northwest Rwanda, Hutu gunmen pointed automatic weapons at the young girls and ordered them to separate into groups of ethnic Hutus or Tutsis. The girls joined hands and refused. Outraged, the gunmen opened fire. Seventeen girls were killed and fourteen were wounded. A month earlier, on March 18, 1997, about twenty gunmen fired automatic weapons and threw grenades at schoolchildren in Kibuye prefecture, south of Gisenyi, killing five pupils. Nineteen others were wounded in that attack, which also occurred after the children refused to separate into groups of Hutus and Tutsis.

Ian O'Gorman, a ten-year-old boy in Oceanside, California, was diagnosed with cancer. The doctors told Ian that he must undergo ten weeks of chemotherapy. They also prepared him for the fact that one of the side effects of the unpleasant process would be the loss of his hair. To avoid the torment of the gradual disappearance, Ian simply had his head shaved at the outset.

When Ian returned to school a few days later, he was met by the thirteen other boys in his fifth-grade class and his teacher. They all had completely shaved heads.

A few challenges:

Think of someone you may have recently slighted. Call and apologize.

Choose one day next week and keep track of how many critical versus encouraging statements you make to colleagues and loved ones.

The next time someone starts to impart gossip, interrupt with, "You know, I think I'd rather not hear about it."

Think of someone you know who is going through a difficult time in his or her life. Imagine what he or she might need right now. Call and offer it.

CHAPTER SEVEN

Self-Control

It is a sad sight. At one of those grand casinos in Las Vegas, a fortyish, suntanned man, in a Ralph Lauren polo shirt and gabardine pleated slacks, sits himself at a blackjack table. His bets at the outset are modest ones. He appears to be having a good time. He chats amiably with the dealer as he experiences the usual ups and downs of the flow of the cards. Then, a sustained losing streak occurs.

His wife, who has apparently been sauntering through the casino, approaches, taps him on the back, and sweetly says, "Hi, honey." The player shrugs off the friendly tap. He is now concentrating intently, his eyes darting back and forth expectantly, from his cards to his "opponent's." Each time he loses, he doubles his previous bet, chasing an illusion. He throws his cards down now in disgust. He is running his hands feverishly through his hair, cursing. At the peak of his exasperation, he flings his losing cards at the dealer. His wife gently tugs on his arm. "Honey, let's go. Tomorrow's another day."

"Leave me alone!" he shouts. "Get away from me! Go up

to the room! Just leave me alone!" She walks off dejectedly. She has witnessed this scene before.

I am at a party and observe the following interaction:

"I think you've had enough to drink," he gently tells her.

"No, I haven't," she slurs in reply.

"Honey, you're not aware that you're . . ."

"Don't tell me what to do!"

"Come on. Let's just go home now. It's getting late, anyhow."

"I will not let you boss me around anymore! You're always trying to control me! You never let me have any fun! Just mind your own business, for once!"

All of this in front of ten friends and acquaintances.

And, finally:

An anorexic-looking woman runs past my friend and me as we walk down my street. I am struck by the intensity in her face. My friend says, "That's Emily. She lives by the elementary school. She runs ten miles, *twice a day*."

For thousands of years, wise men and women have exhorted us to prudence, to moderation. They have understood our propensity to turn a pleasant card game into a test of wills, a drink that relaxes into many that incapacitate, a healthy exercise into one that becomes a compulsion fueled by terror.

Passions, feelings, often lead us astray. You admit, "I know what I *should* do, but . . ." The excuses then tumble out:

But I can't help myself.

But I don't want to.

But I *have* to follow my gut instincts.

But I've denied myself for too long.

But I won't give her the satisfaction.

We usually know what would be good or bad for us. (Even the satisfaction of having "gotten away with something"—an item the checkout person at the grocery store forgot to charge you for, the extramarital encounter you had last week—is usually tinged with some uneasiness. The heart attack that strikes the unfaithful husband during an illicit tryst is not a result of his sexual excitement level having gone off the charts, but rather his guilt feelings that have filled him with anxiety and dread. "Does it make you happy?" is a complex question.) More often than not, the answer to the question, "What's the right thing to do?" is clear. But you simply don't want to do it. Actualizing your higher, moral self requires that you not always do what you feel like doing.

> You have firmly decided to leave your husband. However, you know that he will be receiving a financial windfall in six months. "Should I tell him now, or wait so that I can share the good fortune?" you wonder.

> You have broken up with your girlfriend three times. The last year you were with her felt like one continual heartache and one long headache. You couldn't have a conversation without its deteriorating into an argument. You were betrayed by her brief affair with another man. But you are lonely and miss her terribly. No woman you meet matches her beauty and vibrancy. You remember the great sex, the fun you could have together. You agonize, "Should I try again?"

You pose each of these dilemmas to a friend, and the response you may receive is, "What would make you happy?" or "What do you feel like doing?"

But in both of these cases, "What would make you happy?" or "What do you feel like doing?" are the wrong questions. Feelings are fleeting experiences. Happiness comes and goes. The appropriate questions in these complicated situations are, "What's the right thing to do?" or "What would be the healthiest thing to do?"

We often cringe when we hear, "What's the right thing to do?" The question implies deprivation. Now I can't do what I really want to do. Doing what's right may necessitate the inhibition of momentary impulses. Indeed, we need something to get us through that moment of unbridled desire.

When we turn for guidance to values instead of our feelings, we are more likely to do what is right, fair, just, and healthy. We need rules, we need values, because temptation is everywhere. We have a hard enough time, even when there are guidelines. How many of us have *never* cheated, even a little, on our income tax forms? We call it "stretching the limits," but we know better. (Note the power of self-deception: How many of us consider ourselves felons?)

How many of us have paid a lifelong price for momentary pleasures or passions released uncontrollably? When your spouse finds out about your casual affair, is trust ever fully restored? When your friend betrays a confidence you had entrusted to her, will you ever feel as free to confide again? A patient recently told me about the enduring pain of the insult her husband spat out at her twelve years ago, in a moment of rage. "You're so ugly. I can't bear the thought of having sex with you!" No wonder she felt so unloved. And no wonder she has felt resentment for twelve years.

Momentary feelings or impulses may also obscure what we *really* want.

> Your friend doesn't invite you to his birthday party, so you send him a curt, nasty note demanding that he return the money you loaned him.
>
> Your husband has an extramarital affair, so you decide to "even the score" by having one of your own.
>
> Your boss publicly criticizes you. You lash back by spreading unsavory information to your coworkers about his personal life.

Your impulses lead you to unseemly or even self-destructive behavior. What you really wanted, however, in all three cases, was acknowledgment of how deeply you have been hurt, sincere remorse on the other's part, and some corrective action. "Getting even" may be momentarily satisfying, but will only compound the mess for both of you.

When we live a life dictated by transitory impulses, there is no unified core. Moral decisions demand self-awareness: Who am I? What do I stand for? What do I believe is right? Moral decisions require a firm, moral identity, one that we carry with us from day to day and situation to situation, one that is not so easily tilted by seductive wishes. *Behaving* morally then becomes an act of personal integrity. You demonstrate to yourself and to the world, This is who I am.

The Dangers of Feelings

YOUR CHEERLEADERS HAVE EXHORTED YOU:

Express your feelings!
Get it off your chest! You'll feel better!
Be honest and tell him what you feel!
If you keep it inside, you'll get ulcers or have a heart attack.

But spilling your feelings can be dangerous.

While you express your feelings, you often say things that are irrational and/or untrue. ("You *never* . . ." or "You *always*. . . .")

When you merely express your feelings, your goal is not to negotiate or resolve the problem.

When you are emotionally charged, you often say things that are hurtful. You may say something to me because of a momentary feeling, but I will remember it forever.

When your frustration has mounted, you may rail about something physical, intellectual, or psychological that I cannot do anything about. I will then simply be left with the knowledge of your profound disappointment in me.

We must not take the luxury of merely expressing our feelings without a consideration of the consequences. In fact, the time to talk with me about your anger, your hurt, or your disappointment is when your emotions have cooled. "I want to talk about it now!" you hiss through clenched teeth. But "now!" is the worst time. (When I speak with couples in my clinical practice, I do not simply ask them, "Have you discussed——?" I always want to know, "*How* did you talk about——? What exactly did you say to one another, and how was it said?" In this instance, the "how" and the "when" are just as important as the "what.")

Furthermore, you need not tell me about my every misstep. My oldest daughter, Rachel, recently entered that netherworld of adolescence. If I voiced every irritation, if I responded to every act of insolence, our contact would become one continual battle, and my words would become one continuous stream of criticism. I don't want to do that to her or our relationship.

Oftentimes, we simply *react*. If a driver behind me honks his horn, I will shake my head and think, "Another poor, stressed-out guy." But if I am filled with my own frustrations, I will retaliate. I will honk my horn, or cut him off as he attempts to change lanes. I have now taken his rude behavior personally, even though his impatient blaring had nothing to do with me. He was obviously expressing the letdowns of his life outside of his automobile.

Indeed, when we simply react to perceived slights, we often create unwarranted firestorms. In her book *Anger*, psychologist Carol Tavris relates the following anecdote:

> I was interviewing a thirty-six-year-old dentist who was describing his tranquil life, unmarred by emotional tempests,

when suddenly he blushed over an embarrassing memory. The dentist works out twice a week at a gym near his office, and after vigorous jogging or racquetball it is his custom to go to the "cooling-down" room for flexibility exercises. On this occasion, while he was lifting weights in the cooling-down room, another man accidentally bumped into him. "Why don't you look where you're going, asshole?" the dentist shouted furiously. "Those weights could have fallen on me!" Naturally, the asshole felt it behooved him to reply. Harsher words followed and blossomed into lawsuits. The dentist is sheepish as he tells me the story, for he is no longer angry and wishes he could back out. "I guess I overreacted," he says.

In his *Nicomachean Ethics*, Aristotle wrote: "A person is praised who is angry for the right reasons, with the right people, and also in the right way, at the right time, and for the right length of time."

My patient Norman, a fifty-eight-year-old insurance salesman, certainly failed the "right length of time" test. Three months ago, Norman had broken up (for the second time) with a woman with whom he had conducted a passionate but very tempestuous eighteen-month relationship. Having few friends and no family in Los Angeles, Norman was lonely. He also had a chronic, painful back condition that was at its worst during the past two weeks. Norman's ex-girlfriend heard about his predicament and sent him a note that read, "I know you are having severe back problems. If you need me for anything, I'll be there for you."

Norman's response was propelled by his old anger and present frustrations. "I could never count on you! Remember when we were driving and you called me an SOB?! Remember when you said you'd be there for me after my surgery and all you did was constantly complain about how taking care of me was so draining for you?! Remember when you promised to help me find an apartment and you never even showed up that day?! No, thanks! I know how empty your offer is!" Despite Norman's painful predicament and social isolation, he was unable to accept an extended hand.

Unhappy people hold on to anger. People who are living a fulfilled life push aside memories of old, perceived betrayals. They refuse to be held back by bitterness.

Carol Tavris reminds us that "expressing anger makes you angrier, solidifies an angry attitude, and establishes a hostile habit. If you keep quiet about momentary irritations and distract yourself with pleasant activity until your fury simmers down, chances are you will feel better, and feel better faster, than if you let yourself go in a shouting match." But she nonetheless acknowledges the wisdom of Aristotle's perspective on the expression of anger (or any emotion) when she writes:

> Of course, some experiences of emotional release feel awfully good. Telling off someone you believe has mistreated you is especially satisfying. Publishing the true story of how you were victimized by the bigwigs makes you feel vindicated, especially if the bigwigs are thereby brought to court or to public condemnation. Watching a villain get his comeuppance is a gratification of which we are too often deprived these days. These cathartic experiences do not feel good because they have emptied some physiological energy reservoir, but because they have accomplished a social goal: the redemption of justice, reinforcement of the social order.

As Aristotle emphasized, the questions relevant to the expression of emotion are, When? To whom? In what manner? At what time? and For how long?

The Trouble with Romance

ANGER IS NOT THE ONLY EMOTION THAT FREQUENTLY GETS US INTO trouble. Probably the second most common culprit is sexual or romantic excitement. I am always dumbstruck when I read of couples who marry after knowing one another for a few weeks (or less!). You fall in love for a myriad of possible reasons: "chemistry," sexual passion, a desire to escape loneliness (or insecurity or fear), you want to change the direction of your life, you wish to repair previous psychological damage, you hope you will be loved unconditionally, you have found your "soulmate," you believe the other can make you happy, to name just a few. But whatever needs or desires produced that headlong rush, the initial excitement (some would say delusional) phase of a relationship will soon end. If you and I marry after having known one another for a few weeks, we will be making a lifelong commitment without an inkling of whether our day-to-day, physiologically moderate relationship can withstand the inevitable tremors of our extended future together.

But It's a Once in a Lifetime Opportunity

OFENTIMES, WE ACT HASTILY FOR FEAR THAT WE MAY "MISS OUT." Sitting at a charity luncheon, I overheard part of a conversation between my tablemates, Hal and Ernie. In their mid-forties, Hal and Ernie were real estate investors, and they were discussing a property that had just come on the market.

Hal: "I think it's a great deal. But the seller wants my answer tomorrow, and I haven't had a chance to do a lot of checking."

Ernie: "If you haven't had a chance to thoroughly check it out, then you have to wait. Tell the seller you need a few more days."

Hal: "I know he won't agree. I have to act tomorrow."

Ernie: "You don't *have* to act tomorrow. If he won't give you the extra time, forget about it."

Hal: "But it could be a great deal!"

Ernie: "Hal, there'll be another deal tomorrow. In our business, there are always more deals."

There are few things in life that truly come around only once. Particularly when the stakes are high, don't let your own desperate feelings or other people's pressures push you before you are ready and certain.

Thoughts That Should Be Kept to Yourself

IT IS NOT JUST FEELINGS THAT CAN LEAD US DOWN A DESTRUCtive path. Thoughts may, as well. Or rather, the impulse to disclose your thoughts. Two common examples come to mind: You are married and have sexual fantasies of being with a colleague, friend, or neighbor. You feel guilty about these thoughts. What do these fantasies mean? Should I be honest and tell my spouse about them? you wonder.

Of course, these fantasies are perfectly normal and almost universal. In fact, their complete absence would be surprising. You may want to relieve yourself of some guilt by blurting out your mental tryst, but it won't do your partner a bit of good. No one wants to feel sexually betrayed, even in thought, by a spouse. As with any feeling that prompts disclosure (or action), you must consider the consequences for the other.

The second example often occurs during the dating stages of a relationship. He asks you about past lovers. You answer in vague terms, but he presses you to be more specific. "What was he like?" Hopefully, you know how to choreograph this dance.

What your new love wants to hear is some variation of, "He was very self-absorbed and incredibly selfish. He was not very bright, had no cultural interests, and mostly bored me to death." "And what was your sex life like?" he inquires, hoping you will reply, "It was terrible. He was inept in bed and I soon lost all interest in that area." In the case of previous lovers, if you have wonderful things to say, don't. (Although neutral descriptions would be fine.)

When to Talk and When to Go to Sleep

ALONG THE MINEFIELD OF TOUCHY SUBJECTS, YOU MAY HAVE ALSO learned the importance of correctly *timing* your sensitive conversations. Avoid them when you are very tired. Your defenses will be down, your diplomatic skills will be diminished, and you are likely to blurt out what you had prudently locked away inside you: "I admit it. I am attracted to Marty," or "You're right, I did have an affair with Mandy before I met you," or "It's true. I haven't been interested in sex for a long time. And if you weren't so selfish, I know I wouldn't feel that way because I was always a very sexual person in my previous relationships!"

Avoid potentially touchy subjects when you are tired, stressed, or angry. Otherwise, you will probably say things that are hurtful and exaggerated and can never be retrieved. Should you partner insist, "But I want to talk about it now!," stick to your guns *and* make a future appointment. "I won't talk about it now, but I will talk with you tomorrow night." By now, you can imagine how disastrous the consequences might be if you ever took the position: "I'm going to say what's on my mind whenever I want, and you'll just have to deal with it!"

Don't Take It Out on Me

YOU ALSO DON'T HAVE THE LUXURY OF EXPRESSING YOUR EMOTIONS and then excusing your outrageous, abusive, or irrational behavior by pointing to past debilitating influences. Carly, a thirty-eight-year-old editor of a New Age women's magazine, was telling me about her three-year marriage.

> When Joe withdraws, even if it's for a few hours, I go crazy. He's a pretty thoughtful person, but if he forgets to kiss me good-bye or doesn't call me all day from work, I get depressed. And then when we see each other in the evening, I'm cold and critical. He's a good person. But I'm unhappy with him so much of the time. I find myself yelling at him, and that's just not me.
>
> I know it's old stuff from my past. My father was a withdrawn, unhappy man who was never there for us emotionally. He wasn't at all demonstrative. He never kissed or hugged us. When he was home, he would just sit in front of the television or look at his fishing magazines. I never felt loved by him. I know I'm too sensitive. I know I'm taking out all this stuff on Joe, but it's almost like I can't help myself.

Last week, on a television talk show, an abusive husband nonchalantly explained, "I beat my wife because that's what I saw my father do to my mother."

If your self-control is impaired by overwhelming feelings of deprivation or a response you learned by observing others, you must seek help. The people around you deserve your consideration, not the pus of your festering wounds.

In all this talk of self-control, I do not mean to suggest that you become emotionally constipated. I have run through fields of flowers holding hands with my lover. I have cried when I watched my daughter perform at her ballet recital. I have yelled with the best of them. But when the consequences of our expressions are predictably negative, self-control must be the order of the day.

Dignity derives from actively making choices. Choice implies deliberation. Man is not simply determined by genes or a hurtful past. We always have the free will to do what's right. Aristotle warned that we must restrain the passions that diminish our ability to choose. We must control the fervor that obscures our higher self.

The Quick Fix

SOME THINGS ARE PREDICTABLE. ALLISON, A THIRTY-FOUR-YEAR-OLD attorney who had broken off with her boyfriend three times during the past year and a half, asked me a question, but it was really a plea. "He's been so sweet lately, sending me these loving cards and flowers to the office. He's acting like the guy I fell in love with in the first place. Should I give it another try?" But Allison had "tried" Jerry for five years. Because she was going through that difficult, lonely, pessimistic ("I'll never meet anyone. They're all such jerks out there."), postrelationship period, she wanted relief and hope. "Maybe Jerry's changing." I tell all my patients: The best predictor of future behavior is past behavior. If, for the past five years that Allison has known him, Jerry has been unable to make a commitment, was self-absorbed, work-obsessed, and sexually indifferent, that's probably the way he will be in the future (or at least in the immediate future).

When we are most anxious and deprived, we latch onto a quick fix to relieve our pain. We are not interested in long-term solutions. Even when there is no friend or self-help author urging you, "Be good to yourself!" you reach for that pint of Häagen-Dazs or run out and buy a dress in order to immediately soothe your heartache. How easily the child within sneaks up on us. "I want what I want!" And that primitive, childlike sentiment for immediate gratification fuels your impulsive behavior, for it is only concerned with one issue: "I want to feel good. Now!"

My friend Carol is a very high-ranking executive at a Fortune 500 corporation. A new boss came aboard, with the usual zeal and need to reshape the organization in his image. His abrasiveness and lack of deference to other senior people who had worked there for decades deeply offended my friend. Their relationship deteriorated as his uncollegial behavior persisted. Fairly quickly, Carol simply wrote her boss off and avoided him whenever possible. "I can't even bear to talk with him," Carol fumed.

But Carol's withdrawal was self-destructive. She was probably going to be working with this man for many years. His decisions would directly affect her. She could not afford the luxury of self-righteousness. "You've got to make an effort to have at least a cordial relationship," I urged. So many of us, particularly when we are feeling hurt, anxious, angry, or lonely, find it difficult to appreciate farther-reaching consequences.

Carol lost her balance. When you are driven by only *one* intense emotion, you lose sight of the larger picture. How many of us have been uncontrollably swept away by sexual passions ("I have never been so sexually excited in my life"), anger ("I'll get him back no matter what"), hurt ("I guess I really am worthless"), indignity ("Who does he think he is, coming in suddenly and telling us how to run things?")—so much so that we lose perspective and forget to weigh the multitude of factors that should be relevant. What weight should sexual passion carry in your commitment to a serious relationship? How much will you allow yourself to be *consumed* by your anger? How worthless will you allow yourself to feel because of a rejection? Will you perpetuate a noxious work environment because your boss acts insensitively?

Singularly focused points of view or theories of life can also lead us astray. Remember those individuals who emerged from intensive weekends of EST training, or any of the other simplistic, reductive prescriptions that found favor in the 1960s and 1970s? Remember how robotlike they sounded, spouting the mantras of the keys to happiness, success, and fulfillment? These men and women were on a fixed path with blinders, ones that blocked out any alternative (and certainly any *complex* alternative). Their search had ended. They had found the salve that instantly relieved their hopelessness and uncertainty. (Werner Erhard, the founder of EST, proudly proclaimed to his followers: "You are perfect exactly the way you are." Now there's an appealing sentiment. *I don't have to do anything.* I can just sit back and feel good about myself.) And remember how quickly the "high" of their weekend "revelations" turned southward? When we feel most afraid, we latch onto overly simplified answers because they free us from paralysis. But as you well know, life is far too complex, conflicted, and contradictory to be accommodated by facile, uncomplicated formulas.

We become most primitively reflexive when we feel attacked. When I criticize, your reaction will probably be, "Oh, yeah, well you're not so perfect yourself. Remember when you . . . !" or "Maybe I wouldn't have acted that way if you hadn't . . . !" Your instinct is to retaliate, to assert, "I won't let you get away with that." You bad-mouth me to our mutual boss. So I sabotage one of your favorite projects. I hear that you have spread an unflattering rumor about me. So I gossip about your displays of abject selfishness. But where is this spiral headed? Where will it end? Will it do either of us *any* good?

When you are out of control, you are less than human. When you act like a child who cannot withstand any frustration, you are bound to react unwisely. In either case, your capacity to consider and *choose* from alternatives, your ability to act on your long-term best interest requires that you be wary of any quick fix.

Avoiding Temptation

IN THE COURSE OF OUR CONVERSATIONS, SEVERAL CLERGYMEN OF-fered some variation of, "I leave the door open a bit whenever a female congregant comes to see me. I want to avoid the *possibility* of impropriety." These men of religion are not primarily concerned about spiteful, unfounded accusations of sexual harassment. Rather, they do not entirely trust that their better judgment will be able to contain momentary impulses.

You know your "weak spots." You know the issues or feelings that make it difficult for you to act morally and correctly. Ex-alcoholics don't walk into bars. Ex-compulsive gamblers don't spend weekends in Las Vegas. Ex-addicts don't hang around with old friends who are still using. Women who in the past had been attracted to abusive men hopefully learn to avoid prospective partners who demonstrate telltale signs of that character.

Sometimes, we test ourselves. One of my patients has been struggling with being overweight all of her life. She has had the typical roller-coaster ride of losing pounds with the latest diet fad, and putting them back on just as quickly. At the moment, she was in her thin phase. "Yesterday," she told me, "I walked down the cookie aisle of the supermarket, just to see if I could pass up the Oreos."

But you need not test yourself, especially when you are unsure of your fortitude. You can *anticipate* tempting circumstances and simply avoid them.

We have all been there, especially when we have felt frustrated and needy. All of us have followed an impulse, even though we *knew* it was a dangerous one. Don Gale, a forty-four-year-old attorney, had been suspended by the Bar Association for having sex with a client who was in the midst of a very painful, messy divorce. "Looking back, clearly it was wrong," Don acknowledged. But then he went on, "She was beautiful, and there was real chemistry between us. If I hadn't been her lawyer, and we had met in a different situation, I think we would have hit it off, anyway."

Was Don's perception of "chemistry" accurate? Can we speak of "chemistry between us" when the client is feeling most confused and directionless? Whether we be clergy, attorneys, physicians, or psychotherapists, the rule of no sexual contact with a congregant, client, or patient must be inviolate. Hard and fast rules can help when we are tempted. They can inhibit our tendency to find justification for what we know is wrong. And we must particularly resist the temptation to take advantage of the vulnerable.

You have the ability to think about potential consequences. Knowing yourself, you can anticipate where your frustrations may rear their head and throw you off-balance. When your ego is sagging, you must be careful not to boost it at the expense of another's feelings. (Am I still sexually attractive? Can I seduce her?) When you need to prove something to yourself, do it in a way that does not involve another unsuspecting soul.

Living out a Script

Alice is a forty-one-year-old mother of an eight-year-old boy, and an ex-alcoholic. During one of our sessions, she confessed that she was out of control. "When Billy makes a fuss, I find myself just screaming at him. . . . Sometimes I hit him. . . . I'm aware that it's just what my mother did to me, and that I'm just repeating her behavior. I'm aware of it. And I know Billy is going to hate me for it, just like I hate my mother for what she did to me. . . . I'm aware of it all, but I just can't help myself."

All of us live with hurt, anger, and disappointment. Unfortunately, those who hurt us are often no longer around, and so we take our frustration out on innocent victims. Craig, the stepfather of a ten-year-old girl, explains his sexually abusive behavior: "My father abused me when I was a kid. I guess that's why I did it to her." Too often, we excuse our behavior by pointing to our injured past, as if we are *destined* to live out a script that has been written by another and given to us to enact. Many men and women were abused as children. Most of those individuals did not mimic that abuse with their own sons and daughters. At what point will you simply say, *I am the author of my life!*

At least Alice and Craig recognized past influences upon their present behavior. Many of us, however, have little self-awareness. At twenty-seven, Roger Kimball had already made his millions as an inventor of innovative computer software. As a studious adolescent, Roger had been considered a "nerd" by his classmates. Driven by the usual hormones, he longed for a social life, but was rejected by girls throughout his high school and college years. Then he became rich and famous. His attractive quotient soared. Roger estimated that he had slept with "a couple of hundred" women during the past eight years. "I'm making up for lost time," he jokingly admitted.

But what struck me, early on in therapy, were comments like, "I really like women," or "I like women much more than men. Women are more sensitive, like I am." After a while, I pointed out to him how angry he was with women. ("You use them to prove something to yourself, and then you spit them out.") It took a great deal of discussion before Roger could see it. After all, Roger didn't beat women. On the contrary, he was always gentle, sweet, and attentive. Later in therapy, it became apparent that most of Roger's anger toward women stemmed from the fact that his mother had several affairs while he was growing up. His parents would, unfortunately, fight about those betrayals in front of their children.

Know yourself. Look at your patterns of behavior and do not accept superficial explanations for them. ("I'm just making up for lost time.") Know where you have been hurt in the past, and how those hurts may be manipulating you today.

Do not excuse your actions by referring to old injuries. ("I beat my child because that's what my mother did to me.")

You are responsible for your behavior. If you find it difficult to follow either or both of the above prescriptions, you have an obligation to seek professional help before you snare any more innocent actors into your old scripts.

Are You Happy When I Am Happy?

DID YOU NOTICE THAT YOU HAD TO FORCE YOURSELF TO MARVEL AT the sight of your friend who had recently dropped thirty pounds and looked gorgeous?

Did you notice that you found little pleasure upon hearing from your friend that her daughter received straight A's on her report card?

Did you notice that you became depressed after learning that your friend received a promotion and significant salary increase?

Did you notice that your stomach sank when you finally met your friend's fiancé, a man who lived up to her description of "the most wonderful, intelligent, sexy, and sensitive man on earth."

Did you notice that you were less than thrilled upon reading that your friend sold his first novel for one hundred thousand dollars?

It is difficult to feel good about another's newfound attractiveness when you are feeling insecure about your own. It is difficult to feel good about another child's achievement when your child is struggling. It is difficult to feel good about another's career advancement when you have felt stuck in your position for far too long. It is difficult to feel good about another's fabulous mate when you have focused on the disappointments of your own love life. It is difficult to feel good about another's overnight creative and commercial success when you have been toiling in obscurity for decades. It's just not fair, you feel.

When I feel envy, I resent your having something I am denied. And I also feel as though I have failed. My impotence is highlighted by your triumph.

While envy has been with us since Cain and Abel, I believe it is most prevalent today. It used to be the case that one expected to work hard and "pay one's dues" before reaping the ensuing rewards. But now, we feel *entitled* to a high-paying job, a college education, a luxury car, a sprawling home, and a two-week vacation in Hawaii. If I have them, and you don't, you feel cheated.

Feelings of entitlement and a sense of superiority produce another particularly unseemly reaction. Have you ever noticed that, deep down, you felt some pleasure when you heard that Jim was refused a promotion, when you saw that Sally's boyfriend looked like Howard Stern, or when you read that your friend Mark had lost the race for local councilman? We feel relief when others fail because, at least for the moment, our place in this world's hierarchy is still secure.

Imagine a world where instead of envy, you knew that your friends truly rejoiced in your good fortune. Imagine feeling good enough about yourself and your lot in life so that you could unequivocally share in your friends' happiness.

When we live by a code of morality, by a set of values, we are more likely to feel good about ourselves and our life. Our satisfactions will derive from how we behave, rather than simply from how much we have achieved or acquired. No matter what I have obtained, I can exist peacefully in the knowledge that I have lived correctly. I won't be prone to envy.

You can also help me contain my envy by being sensitive to the discrepancies in our lifestyle, our positions at work, the achievements of our children, our athletic prowess, our physical beauty, or our technical know-how. I can help myself by remembering that "Everyone has their *pekele*," no matter how fine the outside wrapping appears.

During an early session with Brad, a very successful twenty-eight-year-old actor, he bemoaned the fate of those who get what they wish for. "Of course, I have been dying to be where I am now. I always fantasized about being in this position. But I never understood the ramifications. *I have no personal life.* I can't go out to a restaurant. I can't go out on a date without the world knowing about it. I'm a hostage. Photographers camp outside my house! I wouldn't give up the stardom. But I didn't know it would be like this."

We covet another's life or position because we only focus on one side of Rubik's Cube. But it's always a package deal. Brad had fantasized about the fame, the money, the women, and the status. He had not counted on the photographers.

Use your envy to prod you. If you are envious of Joan's figure, resolve to begin an exercise regimen. If you are envious of Michael's creative success, resolve to finally sit down and write, instead of simply talking about all of those imaginative plots. If you are envious of Margie's marriage, resolve to make your own a more intimate and loving one. Put your envy to productive use. Otherwise, envy will only corrode your sense of happiness and satisfaction. You may be resentful at another who has what you want, but your envy only hurts you.

The Man Who Worked at the Ministry of Tourism

IT WAS THE SUMMER OF 1969. I WAS TWENTY AND, WITH MY BACKPACK slung over my shoulder, boarded a plane for my postcollege trip abroad. My jobs as counselor, waiter, and busboy over the past seven summers financed the adventure. At that time, you really could see Europe on five dollars a day. One of the countries I visited was Israel. While there, I met an Israeli woman, Aliza, and we hit it off. Knowing I was alone, she invited me to her parents' for a home-cooked dinner. The apartment, located in a central neighborhood of Jerusalem, was tidy, small, and a bit cramped. I particularly enjoyed speaking with her father, a soft-spoken, gentle man of about sixty, after discovering that we both had family who had lived just a generation previous in the same town in Poland. At one point, I asked him what kind of work he did. He replied, "I work in the Ministry of Tourism." By the modesty of our surroundings, I assumed he was a clerk, or perhaps a lower-level manager.

The next evening, I was in Aliza's Tel-Aviv apartment on Hayarkon Street, overlooking the Mediterranean. The television set was on. Suddenly, an interview with her father appeared on the news. At the bottom of the screen was his name and title, Minister of Tourism. Aliza's father was a Cabinet Minister! Of course, she had a great laugh at the shocked expression on my face. But the incident provided a profound lesson to me in the power of humility. My respect for the man, not the Minister, soared.

The Minister was not playing games with me. He was not attempting to dupe me. He was acknowledging that his title was unimportant. He simply presented *himself* during our lengthy conversation, and that was enough. He let his behavior speak for him.

I have an acquaintance who seizes any opening to press upon me stories of the rich and famous with whom he has dined or partied since we last spoke. He wants to insure that I appreciate his status, as evidenced by the company he keeps. Look at the rarified circles which I am a part of, he insists. I am continually amazed at the number of very accomplished individuals I encounter who still feel compelled to name-drop.

Another acquaintance answers my opening gambit of "What's new?" with a recitation of the latest athletic, academic, or creative awards recently bestowed on his children. My children reflect who I am, he implies. Look at how successful we all are, he suggests.

I notice that when I am feeling insecure, I want the person who introduces me to refer to my "titles." When I want to impress (which occurs as a result of my feeling insecure), I ask the interviewer or journalist to mention that one of my previous books was nominated for the Pulitzer prize. In both instances, I fear that *I* am not enough.

Whether it be obviously done, or more subtly orchestrated (for example, asking another to do it for you), bragging is unseemly. When you brag, you also fail to anticipate my burdens. What if you go on about your high-flying social life, and I am feeling a sense of isolation and a dearth of friends? What if you excitedly tell me of your children's scores in the ninety-ninth percentile, while my sons continue to fail to live up to their academic potential?

Bragging is not merely designed to impress. Bragging is designed to produce envy and assert superiority. It is, therefore, an act of hostility. Bragging is also a transparent ploy. It reveals your lack of self-confidence. "I am not enough," you feel. So you resort to showering me with your "achievements," in order to mask your perceived deficiencies.

Squelch your desire to impress. Let your acts of goodwill, kindness, and sensitivity tell me who you are.

Whether it be acting out of hurt, anger, frustration, inadequacy, *or even good intentions*, we must all be prudent. We must foresee the consequences of our behavior, both for ourselves and for others. Both Plato and Aristotle believed that our lack of self-discipline obscures our impulse to goodness. Gandhi wrote: "A man who is swayed by passions may have good enough intentions, may be truthful in word, but he will never find the Truth."

A few challenges:

In the coming week, think of a pattern of behavior you engage in excessively. Conceive a concrete plan to moderate that behavior. Take an initial baby step to implement the plan.

Think of one behavior you engage in that you know is wrong, but you do anyway. The next time you are tempted to act that way, stop yourself.

The next time you want to retaliate against someone for a perceived slight, offense, or indignity, don't.

SECTION TWO

Strengthening Your Moral Muscle

I T IS MY HOPE THAT THE MORAL PRINCIPLES I HAVE discussed have truly sunk in. One of my goals has been to make you more aware of specific issues such as flattery, bragging, and complaining. But if my book has been successful, you will develop a generally more considerate, sensitive, and fair approach toward everyone with whom you come into contact.

The author and former Catholic monk, Thomas Moore, pointed out: "Nurturing the soul does not mean telling people the right path to clarity and success. It's more about helping them sort out the issues involved." When we are only spoonfed moral rules or lessons, we either embrace them rigidly or we anxiously rebel against them. Mature moral judgment requires active involvement in moral analysis and decision-making. Otherwise, we will be unprepared for *unanticipated* quandaries.

We can sit in armchairs and have theoretical discussions about justice, duty, dignity, and self-control, or we can grapple with problems that occur in the real world. We can mull over the range of possible resolutions to dilemmas, or we can be forced to *choose* a course of action. This section will offer you an opportunity to strengthen your moral muscle by exercising it.

We are often called upon to make moral decisions quickly, under pressure, when we are full of clashing emotions. The more we exercise our moral muscle, the more naturally it will kick in and override feelings and impulses that can lead us astray.

We have all had the experience of having to make a decision with moral implications, but feeling conflicted about it. In other words, confronted with multiple paths that seemed fair or reasonable, we were not completely certain about moving in one direction or another. There were many considerations:

How much should *my* needs count?
What moral principles are at stake here?
With whom do my loyalties lie?
Which moral principles should have priority?
Who needs it more?
Who deserves it more?
At what point am I hurting myself by helping her?
Who can least afford to be hurt?

Even if we have clear moral principles, when we get down to particular cases, our clarity can become blurred. We have moral principles—and we have real life. Moral values are always affected by circumstances. I should be honest. Except when you have been irreparably disfigured and inquire, "Is it difficult for you to look at me?" I should not steal. Except when you are unreasonably and arbitrarily limiting my access to a drug that might cure my son of a life-threatening illness. There is always a *context*, and that context provides dilemmas. Context and principle are always in interplay.

Consider the following: Your sister, Alexis, and Jim are engaged to be married. You find out, through the grapevine, that Jim's previous two marriages ended because of his extramarital affairs. What will you do?

Now, let me add a few elements: (1) Jim is bright, successful, has a good sense of humor, and is very loving with Alexis. (2) While the source of the gossip is a usually reliable one, you cannot verify the information about Jim's past. (3) Alexis is forty, has never been married, and feels desperate to have children.

Before you begin the exploration of your moral self, let me take you through some of my considerations in the scenario involving Alexis, Jim, and their forthcoming marriage.

I don't want to make any precipitous move. The stakes for Alexis and Jim are too high for me to make any hasty decision.

Should I intervene at all? Do I have the right to do anything that might derail the momentum of Jim and Alexis's life?

Are any of my unhealthy needs (such as to be a rescuer, to meddle, to act out old resentments toward my sister) clouding my judgment?

Perhaps I will approach Jim and ask him if the rumor is true. If it is true, why did he have the affairs? Does he believe he will continue this extramarital pattern? If not, why not? Has he told Alexis about this aspect of his history? If not, will I urge him to do so? What good could come of the disclosure?

What if he denies the rumor? Do I have an obligation, nevertheless, to tell my sister what I have heard? What about Jim's right to privacy, particularly against unsubstantiated information? Does my loyalty to Alexis outweigh that principle?

If the information is true, and if there were no extraordinary, mitigating circumstances leading to the affairs, there is a higher probability than usual that Jim will repeat his marital pattern. But it is only a probability. Perhaps the needs that moved him in the past are no longer operative. Perhaps Alexis will provide the missing ingredients that previously drove Jim's frustration, so that he will not feel it necessary to look outside of his marriage. Jim has many fine qualities that should be given weight. Alexis's biological clock is ticking loudly.

If Jim had a future affair, would the marriage survive it? When all is said and done, if Jim had an affair that resulted in the dissolution of the marriage, might Alexis still believe she made the right decision? Should the marriage dissolve, might Alexis be better off moving forward as a single mother, while having taken the risk in marrying Jim because of the love he offered?

Ideally, Jim will have already spoken with Alexis about the affairs in his previous marriages. If that is the case, I would still explore with Alexis her comfort level with that knowledge. Is she being unrealistic when she accepts at face value his declaration, "I would never do that to you!" Is her decision to move forward being overly determined by her desperation of time running out? Of course, with all of the facts at hand, ultimately this is Alexis's decision to make. But I can help her look at all sides of the dilemma.

In your own life, you will never confront all of the scenarios presented in this section. However, do not pass up the dilemmas that seem foreign or irrelevant to you. They provide an even greater challenge for you to stretch your imagination. One of the best ways to activate your empathic abilities is to role-play, to adopt another's frame of reference, to understand the desires and frustrations that move him.

When considering moral dilemmas, you must be concerned about all the parties, and you must weigh their competing interests. In many cases, you will have to come to peace with the fact that you will not be able to make everyone happy. There is often no rational way to objectively weigh the claims of one loyalty or principle against another. This section of the book is not a test. It is not about arriving at the "correct" answer. It is, rather, a voyage of discovery: What do I stand for? Which values are most important to me? Who am I?

In approaching the scenarios, it would be helpful to follow these guidelines:

Recognize that there is a moral dilemma. Refrain from rushing to judgment. If the right path seems obvious to you, force yourself to more closely examine the competing claims and the motives of all the actors.

Examine your own fears, insecurities, resentments, and prejudices that might get in the way of making the right choices.

Understand what each actor wants. What drives him or her? What's going on in his or her life? Think about how each actor would want to be treated.

Consider the context. What information would you like to collect that might inform your decision? What situational variables might be relevant in assessing the merits of each course of action?

Decide what values should have priority. Where do your loyalties lie? Where do your responsibilities lie?

NOTE: If you believe a scenario lacks sufficient detail or is unclear, make an assumption that will correct the problem. Also, in Dilemmas 1, 2, 4, 6, 8, 10, 13, 16, 17, and 21, you may reverse the gender if that will allow it to feel more personally meaningful.

You may want to utilize these dilemmas simply as an opportunity for introspection. If that is the case, do not explore more than one a day. I want your approach to be a thoughtful one, not a rushed one. I want you to ruminate about the issues involved.

On the other hand, you may want to explore the dilemmas with others. Instead of polite social conversation, a group discussion of the principles involved can provide a vehicle for getting to know one another in a deeper, more intimate way. Your friends or acquaintances may, at first, be wary of your suggestion. But most of us hunger for more honest and meaningful interaction. You can help the others feel safe enough to enter the discussion by your own willingness to be candid and forthright.

Dilemma 1

You are a firefighter with a wife and two children at home. While dealing with a blaze that is threatening a newly built commercial development, you hear on the radio that an edge of the firestorm is quickly approaching your house. What will you do?

What if the blaze you are fighting is threatening homes where other families live?

Dilemma 2

You have been struggling to make ends meet for several years. Because you were once married to a famous, flamboyant actress, a publisher approaches and offers you a great deal of money (enough to clear up all of your debts and live comfortably for several years) to write a book about your tempestuous years together. He makes it clear that he expects you to include all "the juicy details." When you voice some hesitation, he adds, "It was a part of your life together. It happened. You're not making it up. In fact, you would be less than honest if you left it out." What will you do?

What if the two of you had children who are now adults?

Dilemma 3

Your twenty-year-old nephew who has been backpacking around the country arrives unexpectedly on your doorstep. He has a high temperature, chills, and a very peaked look on his face. He asks if he can stay with you for a couple of days until he recovers. He knows no one else in the city. Your own ten-year-old child has just fully recovered from a severe case of pneumonia and, since birth, has been afflicted with a weak heart that can be adversely affected by any illness. What will you do?

What if your nephew's mother (your sister), who is ten years older than you, had virtually brought you up after your own mother died at a young age?

What if you and your nephew's mother have been estranged from one another for many years?

Dilemma 4

Your mother is eighty years of age and no longer able to care for herself. She clearly expects you to invite her to live in your home. Whenever the subject of a retirement residence comes up, her response is, "I'd rather not live than be in one of those places." Your wife and your mother have always had a tense relationship. Your wife makes it clear that she does not want your mother to move in. What will you do?

What if your mother is always very critical of your two teenage daughters?

What if your mother and two teenage daughters get along fabulously?

What if your mother-in-law, whom you do not get along with, is frail, alone, and also making comments about how she would like to live in your home when she can no longer care for herself?

Dilemma 5

You are a lawyer who bills your time at two hundred and fifty dollars an hour. Your next-door neighbor, Jim, is an electrician who bills his time at sixty dollars an hour. Jim asks you to do ten hours of legal work for him. In exchange, he offers to do ten hours of electrical repair work that you need in your home. Is this arrangement acceptable to you? If not, what would you propose?

Dilemma 6

You have been married to Beth for twenty years. You have no children together. Beth has a nervous breakdown, and her personality has been transformed from the outgoing and witty woman you loved to a depressed and completely withdrawn soul. After two years of therapy, she has shown no improvement, and the doctors do not know when, to what extent, or if she will ever recover. You are only forty and feeling the frustration of the lack of companionship. What will you do?

What if you have children together?

Dilemma 7

Recently married, you and your spouse simultaneously graduate law school. You each receive "an offer of a lifetime" from very prestigious firms. The only problem is that the jobs are in cities that are three thousand miles apart. What will you do?

Dilemma 8

You and your wife divorce after fifteen years of marriage. You have an offer of an interesting and very financially rewarding job in another city, a thousand miles away. Your son is thirteen and your daughter is ten. They are both obviously shaken by the breakup. What will you do about the job offer?

What if your divorce has been a very acrimonious one, and the town you live in is small enough so that you frequently come into contact with your ex?

Dilemma 9

You are a physician and your patient has inoperable, fatal cancer. He has, at most, six months to live. You also know that optimism is both psychologically and physically helpful for coping with this illness. What will you tell him?

What if you had, once before, been sued for "lack of full disclosure" to a patient?

Dilemma 10

Both you and your husband have been atheists. Your husband, however, recently found God, and the two of you now disagree strongly about how religiously observant your family (which includes two children) should be. What will you do?

What if one of your children develops a potentially fatal illness?

Dilemma 11

Over the year you have lived in the building, you have often run into the couple next door, the Smiths. They are usually holding hands and very sweet with one another. One evening, you hear shouting and crashing noises from their apartment. You knock on the door. Mrs. Smith, a gash over her right eye seeping blood, opens it and says, "Mind your own business." What will you do?

Dilemma 12

Without a kidney transplant, your best friend will die in one month. Your kidney is a perfect match for his. If you donate your kidney, the odds of your survival to a normal life span is 50-50. You have two children. What will you do?

Dilemma 13

Your marriage of fifteen years is a fairly good one. On a scale from one to ten, you would rate it a seven. You meet someone who is your absolute soulmate, someone whom you are certain would bring you a lifetime of passion, fun, and profound closeness. He tells you that he is not interested in an affair, but would love to be with you if you were free of your marriage. You have two children who are in their teens. What will you do?

Dilemma 14

Your two best friends are a married couple, Joanne and Bill. One day, you spot Joanne having lunch with a man who is unfamiliar to you. He is holding her hand during much of the lunch, and when they part, they embrace. Bill has been telling you for months about his suspicions that Joanne is having an affair. Joanne has repeatedly denied to him any such relationship, and because of Bill's great trust in her, he believes the denial. Over coffee, Bill tells you, "I think my imagination is driving me crazy. There must be something very wrong with me." What will you do?

What if you had an extramarital affair five years ago that you kept hidden from your spouse?

Dilemma 15

Your close friend, Arthur, asks you to lie for him during a legal proceeding. In other words, he asks you to commit perjury. You know that his lawsuit has merit, and that the other party, Ralph, blatantly cheated Arthur while they were business partners. However, Ralph's attorneys have been extremely adept at painting a favorable picture of their client. Your lie may be the only way for Arthur to win his case. What will you do?

What if you know that Ralph committed perjury during the proceedings?

Dilemma 16

Your close friend, Paul, is applying for a critical job on a research team that is trying to find the genetic contribution to a particular form of cancer. He asks you for a letter of recommendation, and because of your reputation in the field, it could be decisive in determining whether he gets the position. However, you have reservations about whether your friend is the best qualified for the undertaking. What will you do?

What if Paul helped your wife obtain a job last year?

Dilemma 17

You have been married for five years. Your marriage has been a close, supportive, fun-filled, and affectionate one. Your spouse says she would like to have a child. You are happy with the way things are and have never particularly felt a desire to have children. You and your spouse have never discussed the subject before, always deferring with, "We'll see how we feel." But now, she is sure she wants to start a family, and you are equally sure you don't. What will you do?

What if she accidentally becomes pregnant?

Dilemma 18

A man was sentenced to prison for three years after he was found guilty of embezzlement from a charity. One year into his sentence, he escaped, moved to a different part of the country, and took on a new identity. For five years, he worked hard in construction and gradually saved enough to start his own business. He was fair to his customers, gave his employees top wages, and gave most of his profits to charity. One day, you recognize him from an article in the news-paper on escaped convicts who are still at large. What will you do?

What if he was originally convicted of kidnapping and sentenced to prison for fifteen years?

What if his business is so big that the town's economy depends on it?

Dilemma 19

Your neighbor of twelve years, Tom, experienced the failure of his business six months ago and is presently in the midst of a divorce. Over the years, your children have played together, and you have shared an annual Fourth of July barbecue together. You have always wanted a larger house such as the one Tom owns. The house is listed for sale at two hundred thousand dollars, which is a fair market price. But a broker tells you, "I know Tom is in a financial bind. You can get it for much less if you make an offer now." What will you do?

What will you do if you can't afford to pay more than $175,000?

Dilemma 20

You are about to graduate law school and have interviewed for several jobs. An offer comes in from James and Parker, a very good firm. However, they tell you they must have an answer by tomorrow. You hesitate because James and Parker is your second choice and you have not yet heard from Monroe and Monroe, the firm you most want. When you call Monroe and Monroe to tell them about your bind, they inform you that they will not be making any decisions until the following week, and that there have been many fine applicants for their opening. Given the uncertainty of the situation, you decide to accept the offer from James and Parker, which means that they will send rejection letters to the other applicants. The next week, Monroe and Monroe call to extend an invitation to join their firm. What will you do?

Dilemma 21

You have promised your daughter, Jenny, a car for her seventeenth birthday. Jenny is a wonderful kid—compassionate, studious, creative, and generous. But she is also very insecure and, therefore, very conscious of the approval of her peers. You offer to buy her a modest, used car. She comes to you in tears the next day: "My two best friends are both getting a new car. Daddy, can I *please* have a new one, too?" Your values tell you that it is a bit unseemly for a seventeen-year-old to have a new car. (After all, you were in your mid-twenties when you purchased your first new car, and you bought it with your own money.) It is also the case that you have done very well financially in recent years and could easily afford the purchase. What will you do?

Dilemma 22

You are a personnel manager at a company that has been forced to tighten its belt. The president of the company orders you to cut two people from a team of four that is working on the development of a new product. Two of the individuals on the team, Mark and Sheilah, have been with the company for fifteen years. Sheilah is a single mother with two young children. The other two members of the team, both single individuals in their twenties, were hired within the past three years. They are both a bit more dynamic and creative than the two senior personnel. What will you do?

Dilemma 23

You are at work and, over lunch, a colleague says, "I can't believe what I just found out about Bob Bailey!" Bob Bailey is competing with your brother, Albert, for a promotion. Albert is more competent than Bob and deserves the new position, but Bob is a favorite of the boss. The damaging information you hear about Bob's personal life could insure that Albert gets the job if it were ever leaked to the boss. What will you do?

Dilemma 24

You have carpooled to work with Dan for five years. When you were down on your luck, Dan, a longtime neighbor, recommended you for a job at the company where he worked and urged you to apply for it. One day, as you arrive at the office, Dan scrapes another door as he gets out of the car. He says nothing and believes that you are not aware of the damage he has caused. The next day, a coworker, Pam, announces at a staff meeting that her car door was scratched badly and she would like to know who did it. What will you do?

Dilemma 25

Your business is sinking, and your partner approaches you with an idea. He wants to take a piece of office equipment and put it in a different box that has a brand name on it. The cheaper office equipment looks exactly like the brand name, so the consumer will never know the difference. Furthermore, all consumer tests have shown no difference in the quality, even though they are made by different companies, and the one with the brand name has a considerably higher retail price. This strategy your partner suggests will allow your company to stay afloat. Your partner also reminds you that you have twenty employees, most of whom support a family, and that the job market is very tight. What will you do?

Dilemma 26

You are a surgeon. Two patients require a liver transplant, but there is only one liver available. One patient is a forty-year-old father of two young children whose liver was destroyed by his longtime excessive consumption of alcohol. The other patient is a seventy-seven-year-old widow with no history of having abused her body. What will you do?

Dilemma 27

Hundreds of thousands of people in America go to bed hungry at night. How do you feel about spending large sums of money on luxury items for yourself? Should the enormous number of needy people affect how you spend your money?

Dilemma 28

A seventy-one-year-old grandmother, who had never been in trouble with the law, attempted armed robbery of a gas station. During the attempt, her gun went off accidentally, injuring the attendant. Relatives say she was distraught over a foreclosable debt on her home and an IRS lien on her husband's Social Security check. Assume you are the judge. What will you decide in this case?

Dilemma 29

Would you turn in a member of your family or a close friend if you believed he or she was involved in a serious crime?

Would it matter to you if the person was married and had young children?

Would the nature of the crime matter to you? For example, if the crime was armed robbery versus embezzlement?

Dilemma 30

You are instructing your teenagers about the dangers of sex and drugs. Your child asks you if you had sex or did drugs when you were his age. Assume you had. What will you tell your child?

In order to fully appreciate the role context plays in moral decision-making, go back to a few of the previous scenarios that you easily resolved and add a factor that would make your choice a more difficult one.

Make up your own scenarios. Be sure that the principles in conflict are weighty ones—justice, conscience, loyalty, honesty, compassion, etc.

SECTION THREE

Strengthening Your Child's Moral Muscle

W E MAY HAVE THE CAPABILITY OF REASONING in a morally mature manner, but needs, emotions, and external pressures can cause any of us to view circumstances in a simpler, more self-interested light. We may have advanced moral judgment, we may embrace high moral principles, and still not behave in a moral fashion.

But we can direct our children onto the right path.

We can reinforce their emotional reactions that support compassion and moral behavior.

We can foster a respect for authority and an attention to the needs of the social order (such as family or community) that supersede personal interest.

We can make firm demands on our children while remembering to follow those demands with their underlying justifications, instead of simply bellowing orders. We can teach not only what is wrong, but why it is wrong.

We can make distinctions in our concern between rules for good manners and household order, and issues of moral substance affecting justice and human relations.

We can insure that our children participate in the kinds of social experiences (such as helping the needy and having contact with those less fortunate) that will nurture their nascent moral sensibilities.

We can, by our own actions, let our children know that we care about other people.

We can continually encourage our children to put themselves in another's shoes.

We can take the time to engage them in discussions of hypothetical moral conflicts.

Children need to be recognized for acting morally. Catch your child being good, and reinforce that behavior. Make concrete suggestions to your children that reflect kindness, generosity, and justice. For example, offer options for reparations when your child has acted cruelly or inconsiderately.

How can I emphasize this enough? The closer the relationship, the stronger the bond you have with your child, the more influential you can be. Of course, our sway over our sons and daughters will diminish as they get older. Certainly, during adolescence, their peers will dominate their life. But we should not use this development as an excuse to retreat from our responsibility to be a moral guide. The building blocks of a moral self that we can help our children forge early on will determine how susceptible to or autonomous from the pressures of those around them they will be.

We are locked in a battle with alluring advertising, silly television, obscene music, rampant substance abuse, and the seduction of the easy life. We are attempting to blunt the force of a culture that prizes money and material possessions above the moral life. We are fighting for the souls of our children.

Our sons and daughters are watching us. They are acutely sensitive to inconsistencies between what we advise and what we do. Our lessons will always be undermined by our contrary behavior.

Our children are observing our everyday generosities and our everyday dishonesties. Don't expect your children to be better than you. Perhaps out of rebelliousness, perhaps simply out of desire to avoid an obligation, your children will immediately pick up on your hypocrisies. ("How could you tell me to——when you——!") When there is a discrepancy between what is practiced and what is preached, it makes sense that the observer will take the easier road.

Give your children a role to which they can aspire.

All of us want our children to be moral. We would all agree that children should be honest, kind, fair, responsible, and respectful of social rules and authority. As parents, we want to see our children develop into independent individuals who are concerned for others and who think for themselves. Moral issues such as abortion, sexual orientation, censorship, and welfare may divide us. But in our most fundamental dreams for our children's morality, we hold similar goals and visions. We want our sons and daughters to become good people.

How do they develop the foundations of morality?

The American psychologist Lawrence Kohlberg and the Swiss psychologist Jean Piaget have been the most influential theoreticians of moral development. Both concluded that moral judgment develops through a series of cognitive reorganizations called stages. And each stage, they believed, has an identifiable, consistent pattern of thinking. In other words, if you can identify which stage the child has entered, you can predict how he will think about moral problems.

Kohlberg and Piaget assume that we are inherently motivated to determine what is right and what is wrong. Both psychologists proposed that all of us move through the same series of stages of moral reasoning, which are qualitatively different from one another. The sequence is true for both males and females, and for all cultures.

However, while all of us move through the stages in the same order, we do not progress at the same pace, nor do we all progress as far.

The development of moral judgment requires the parallel maturation of cognitive abilities. For example, around the age of seven, most children are able to make inferences, and by age twelve, adolescents can reason abstractly, form hypotheses, and deduce implications from them. As cognitive abilities mature, moral thinking can also become more sophisticated. Both cognitive and moral development require a supportive environment. While the biological structure is genetically programmed to unfold from within, we can stimulate the progress by nourishing the capability, or we can retard the process by our neglect.

A child moves from what we call a conformist morality to an altruistic morality. At first, he defers blindly to authority and to the rules imposed on him. He is aware that these rules do not necessarily reflect his underlying feelings, but he is motivated simply by the self-interest of avoiding punishment for disobedience.

At about the age of three, he develops the ability to step outside of himself. He realizes that his feelings of hurt, anger, and distress at being unjustly treated are also felt by others when they are transgressed against. Adults can foster this empathic process by prodding the child, "How do you think your behavior made Jennifer feel?" The sine qua non of moral behavior is the ability to take the viewpoint of another.

For Lawrence Kohlberg, former professor at the University of Chicago and Harvard University, when the child begins the *preconventional level* of moral reasoning, he believes everyone sees the world as he does. The fact that other people have different interests, perceptions, or desires is neither recognized nor considered. He renounces selfish impulses in simple response to offered rewards and threatened or imposed punishment. As he moves further through this level, an awareness of other points of view emerges and he adopts a very pragmatic approach to the resolution of conflict: I'll do this for you, if you do that for me. Reciprocity is a matter of "you scratch my back, and I'll scratch yours," not of loyalty, gratitude, or justice.

For the preconventional child, rules and social expectations are something external to the self. At the next, *conventional level*, the child (around the age of nine) begins to value and internalize the expectations of his family and community, regardless of the immediate consequences for him. He pledges his allegiance to the social order and identifies with those who impose it.

During the *postconventional level*, the person struggles with defining moral values apart from what authorities have laid down. He tries to answer the questions, What is right? and What is wrong? for himself. Aside from accepting the procedural rules of the group (for example, how to resolve conflict, when to honor agreements), right becomes a matter of personal values and opinions. By the end of this stage, while his conscience and personal ethics drive his moral judgment, abstract principles of universality and consistency are also appreciated.

It is the way we think about issues that determines our moral maturity. Although Kohlberg asserted that we all go through the given sequence of stages, those stages are not age-specific. Some adults never advance beyond a very early stage of reasoning. While one grown-up may think cheating is wrong because it undermines the trust necessary for social cohesion, another may simply believe it should be avoided because you can get caught and punished if you do it.

Kohlberg marshaled evidence for this theory from six different cultures, both Eastern and Western—the United States, Turkey, Taiwan, Great Britain, the Yucatan, and Mexico. Although the stage-development notion or *structure*-of-thinking approach maintains the same sequence in these diverse countries, contemporary cultural norms influence the *content* of ideas. Content, which is formed by experience, tells us *what* a person believes, while structure tells us *how* a person thinks about the content of his beliefs. Content is determined by context. So, Kohlberg wrote, "Socrates was more accepting of slavery than was Lincoln, who was more accepting of it than Martin Luther King."

Jean Piaget, the former codirector of the Institute of Educational Science in Geneva and professor of experimental psychology at the University of Geneva, focused his work on children between the ages of six and twelve and identified two broad stages of moral reasoning within that group. Younger children are at the stage of *heteronomy*. Their rules for behavior have been externally imposed by authority figures. The prohibitions against damaging property, lying, or stealing are not seen as necessary for the continued, smooth functioning of the group, but are simply perceived as arbitrary and inflexible ones, "laid down by the gods."

The stage of heteronomy gradually gives way to the idea that rules are more flexible. Children focus less on punishment as an inhibitor of transgression, and more on issues of trust and fairness when explaining why it is wrong to steal, cheat, or lie. Before the age of seven, consequences, not intent, determine the degree of guilt. The child is harshest in his judgment of the one who has done the most damage. But then, intent takes on greater significance. Who is worse, a child who broke five bowls by accident while carrying them for his mother, or a child who broke one bowl while playing with it after having been told not to touch it? The older child is more likely to find the second situation worthy of condemnation.

The preferred form of that condemnation changes as well for the older child. He increasingly rejects arbitrary punishment (such as spanking) in favor of reciprocity-based punishment that either does to the culprit as he did to others, allows the offender to suffer the natural adverse consequences of his actions, or requires him to make restitution.

While children may go through identifiable stages of moral development (albeit at different paces), it is clear that they act more morally in some relationships or situations than others. They may be more truthful with a friend than a parent, for example. It is also the case that the salient moral principle may differ depending on the perspective of the child and the adult. When a child "covers" for a friend who is doing what he is not supposed to be doing, the prominent issue for the child is loyalty, not honesty. Perhaps it is most important to remember that a child's *temperament* and *impulse control* will not only affect his ability to "think through" complex dilemmas, but also his ability to follow through on what even he believes is the right course of action.

Morality must not remain simply theoretical, either for ourselves or for our children. Our goal, as parents, is to help our children when we are not around. By involving them in moral dilemmas, both our own and theirs, both real-life and fictitious, they will be able to respond to inevitable occasions of conflict when they arise. Morality will become a part of their character so that they will be able instinctively to make the right choices.

This section presents moral dilemmas for you to discuss with your children. They are divided into ones suitable for elementary-school-age youngsters, and those more appropriate for adolescents. If you present this exercise as an opportunity to play games with their imagination, you will find that your sons and daughters will leap into the fray. Be sure that you not only ask your children, "What is the right thing to do?" but also, "*Why* is that the right thing to do?" They must learn to articulate the rules they employ to resolve the dilemmas. As was the case for adults in the preceeding section, do not tackle more than one dilemma at a sitting. Allow the richness and importance of the material the time to sink in and take hold.

Moral education programs can stimulate moral faculties. Experience has shown, however, that information-laden courses are not nearly as effective as those that promote discussion. If you are a teacher, scout leader, clergyman, coach, or are involved in any other role where you have access to groups of children, you may find it most productive to bring these dilemmas up for examination among several boys and girls at once.

For Younger Children

It is your birthday, and you bring candy to school to share with everyone. But your best friend, Bob (Mary), does not want you to give any candy to one of your classmates, Tim (Sally), because Tim (Sally) has been mean to him (her). What will you do? Why will you do that?

Your friend Sharon (Jim) asks you to steal a pen for her (him) because she (he) is poor and does not have one. What will you do? Why will you do that?

There is a club that meets after school and is a lot of fun. There is only one space left for another child to join. Pretend you are the leader of the club. Your best friend asks you if she (he) can join. She (he) is very unhappy because she (he) does not have many friends. But there is another girl (boy) who has been waiting much longer to join and is first on the waiting list. What will you do? Why will you do that?

Your friend Gloria (Graham) is too sick to finish her (his) science fair project so she (he) asks you to help her (him). There is a rule that says everyone must do the project by herself (himself). What will you do? Why will you do that?

Pretend that you are walking home with your brother, Henry, and you fall and cut your leg. You and Henry go to a nearby store and ask the owner if you can call your parents. The store owner says you have to pay to use the telephone. But you don't have any money. You notice that Henry steals the money while the owner is not looking. What will you do? Why will you do that?

You want to play with your friend, Roger (Roberta). But Howard (Helen) does not have any friends and asks you to play with him (her). What will you do? Why will you do that?

Your sister let you play with some of her toys yesterday. Today, she tells you that she wants to play with your very favorite toy, which you don't want to share with anyone. What will you do? Why will you do that?

Your mother tells you never to ride your bicycle in the street at night. But one night, your friends are riding their bicycles in the street at night and you join them. The next day, your mother tells you that a neighbor thought she saw you riding your bicycle in the street last night but she wasn't sure that it was you. Your mother wants to know if the neighbor is correct. What will you tell your mother? Why will you do that?

For a long time, you have really wanted a certain toy. But your parents told you that you have to wait until you save ten dollars so you can buy it with your own money. One day, you are walking down the street and see a wallet on the ground. It has twenty dollars in it. What will you do with it? Why will you do that?

You are with three of your friends and they are all making fun of Gary, who they think is a real jerk. You don't have any feelings about him because you don't really know him. Your friends keep asking you, "Don't you think Gary's a jerk?" What will you do? Why will you do that?

Your two friends take a really great color marker from the teacher's desk, even though they know they are not supposed to. They tell you to take one too, because the teacher has so many markers that she won't even notice. Also, your teacher has been really mean to the class the whole week. What will you do? Why will you do that?

Your friend Alex is very poor. One day, he tells you he is hungry because he has had nothing to eat for two days. While the two of you are walking, you pass a bakery. Alex goes inside, and while no one is watching, he steals some bread and leaves the shop. What will you do? Why will you do that?

One day you come home and tell your parents that you got a very good grade on a test. But it is not true. Your mother wants to reward you because she believes you did so well on the test, so she offers to buy you a new toy. What will you do? Why will you do that?

Your mother tells you and your two brothers that you should not play with her scissors while she is out. But when she leaves the house, your two brothers take the scissors and begin to cut some drawing paper. Your brothers tell you to use the scissors also, but you say you don't want to. When your mother comes home, she sees the cut-up paper on the floor and wants to know who did it. What will you do? Why will you do that?

You and your friend start throwing snowballs at each other. Your friend throws one and accidentally breaks a window in a house. The owner of the house comes out to find out what happened. What will you do? Why will you do that?

Yesterday, your brother was really mean to you. Today, your brother is sick, so your mother asks you to clean up both your room and his. What will you do? Why will you do that?

Make up a situation where what you want to do is different from what your friend wants to do. What will you finally decide? Why will you decide to do that? How will you feel if you don't get to do what you want? How will your friend feel if she (he) doesn't get to do what she (he) wants?

For Adolescents

Your close friend, Jill (Jack), has a crush on David (Amy). David (Amy), however, does not have any feelings about Jill (Jack.) David (Amy) asks you out on a date, and you like him (her) a lot. What will you do? Why will you do that?

It is very important to your parents that you go to church (or synagogue) regularly. However, you are not sure if there is a God. What will you do? Why will you do that?

You don't want to have sex with your boyfriend (girlfriend), and he (she) does. You love him (her) and want him (her) to be happy, but you don't feel you are ready to take that big step. What will you do? Why will you do that?

The night before an important test at school you had to take care of your sick father, and so you didn't have the time to study. You had been doing well in the class all year. The following day, when you get the test, there are a lot of questions you are unable to answer. However, you are sure that if you had been able to study the night before, you would have been able to answer most of those questions. During the test, the teacher leaves the room for a while and you have an opportunity to cheat from the smart student sitting next to you. What will you do? Why will you do that?

On Monday, you get an invitation to Barbara's party, which will be on Saturday night. You call her and tell her you will be coming. On Thursday, you get an invitation to Sherry's party, which will also be on Saturday night. You would rather go to Sherry's party because more of the "cool" kids are going to be there. You can't go to both because they are too far from one another. What will you do? Why will you do that?

Your friend Roy is doing drugs. Roy's schoolwork is going downhill, and he almost got into a terrible car accident one day because he was driving while he was high. You know that Roy would be really angry if you told his parents about his drug use, but you are also afraid that Roy's life is falling apart. What will you do? Why will you do that?

You are with your two best friends and they are making fun of Jordan, who they think is a real nerd. You don't have any feelings one way or the other about Jordan, but your friends keep asking you, "Don't you think Jordan's such a nerd?" What will you do? Why will you do that?

You are having a party. You invite your friend Helen (Mark). Then, Arlene (Adam), your *best* friend, says she (he) won't come if Helen (Mark) is there because they had a big fight last week. What will you do? Why will you do that?

You are at a party, and your friends are drinking beer. You don't like the taste of beer, and when you tried it once before, it made you nauseous. But your friends keep insisting that you have some so you can really "join the party." Everybody seems to be having fun, and you feel a little awkward being the only one not drinking. What will you do? Why will you do that?

The most popular girl in your class, Jenny, asks you to do her a big favor and write a school report for her. She is going on vacation for a week with her parents, and she says she won't have the time to do it herself. You don't have many friends, and this could be your way to get involved with the "in" crowd. What will you do? Why will you do that?

Your parents go away for the weekend and tell you not to drive their new car. But when your friends come over, they are dying to go for a ride in it because it is so luxurious. You believe that no one will ever find out if you drive it. What will you do? Why will you do that?

Your older sister has been really mean to you all week. One day, you go into her room to see if your CD is in there. You find your CD, and then you notice her diary lying on her bed. You're dying to read it. What will you do? Why will you do that?

Last month, you made a commitment to help serve dinner at a homeless shelter this coming Friday night. But now your friend invites you to a party for that same night, and you really want to go. He calls you and says, "Blow it off. Just tell them you can't come and that you'll do it another time." What will you do? Why will you do that?

Think about a moral dilemma (something involving issues of right and wrong) you recently experienced where you had to decide whether you would help someone who is important to you.
What was the situation?
What moral issues were involved?
What options did you consider?
Why did you choose the option you did?
Do you think you did the right thing? Why? (If not, why not?)

Think about a moral dilemma you recently experienced—something involving lying, or cheating, or stealing, or fairness, or loyalty.

State the point of view of each person involved in the situation.

What did you think were the moral issues involved?

What options did you consider? What were the pros and cons of each? Why did you accept or reject the options?

Looking back to that time, do you think you did the right thing? Why? (If not, why not?)

Epilogue

Wouldn't it be comforting to know that there are good, honest, kind people at our workplace, driving in their cars, repairing our appliances, negotiating our contracts, living next door, or caring for our sons and daughters?

But we are all like children, frightened of being deprived, angry at anticipated unfairness. Your generosity of spirit can help us reject our selfish selves and embolden us to act from our compassionate, considerate, benevolent selves.

You may ask, "What impact can I have in a universe that behaves so insensitively, so unkindly, so immorally?" The Rabbi of Ger told his followers that, when he was a young man, he wanted to change the world. By the time he reached middle age, he only wanted to influence his community and those around him. In old age, he realized that what was most important was to change himself.

Start with yourself. The world will follow. For when you are better, you will assuredly affect me. You will calm my fears and encourage the best within me to emerge. You will stoke my courage to do what is right.

As a clinical psychologist, I find myself using the word *courage* more and more with my patients. I invite them to be courageous, both because it is empowering to overcome fears, and because it is heartening to observe oneself act justly.

To have moral integrity is to have an emotionally compelling sense of oneself. Self-respect, then, precludes certain actions. It might involve the conscious choice of not cutting into the front of the line despite the fact that no one would notice. Or the force of one's moral sense might prompt one to take a stand that could even be self-injurious. In *A Man for All Seasons*, the Duke of Norfolk implores Thomas More to save his life by swearing to the oath declaring Henry VIII the head of the Church of England. More tells the Duke: "I will not give in because I oppose it—*I* do—not my pride, not my spleen, nor any other of my appetites, but *I* do—*I!*"

At the end of the day, you want your life to mean something. You can make a lot of money, accumulate a bunch of toys, achieve a certain status, or experience the natural wonders of the world. But then what? How will you fill the void? What will incite you?

As you focus on your higher self, your moral self, you can transform your being by shifting your goals. You won't have to ache to be "somebody." You can just be yourself, a self committed to kindness and generosity. You won't have to envy others, because what you strive for will be within your grasp.

So many of us today feel alone, isolated. "Whom can I really count on?" we lament. We can connect with our neighbors, our colleagues, our friends, and our family by recognizing our moral obligations to them. We can discover a sense of continuity that will bind us to future generations by providing them a moral foundation upon which to build. We can shine a guiding light for our children and their children to come.

Take a look at the face, the posture of people who are rude, selfish, critical, competitive, inconsiderate, or unfair. Observe those who are pushing people out of the way, both literally and figuratively, instead of extending a hand. When we act from our frightened selves, we reinforce our fears. We may marshal justifications for our unseemly acts, but those excuses are insufficient to completely mask our uneasiness. We look at our behavior and know we have failed.

For those of you who routinely act from your moral self, please keep it up. I need your example. For those of you who have stumbled, the past is gone. Resolve to do better, starting now. A long time ago, Plato observed that acting immorally inevitably brings unhappiness.

Be happier, be good.

Acknowledgments

I would like to thank Diane Henschel, Joe Viola, and my wife, Rebecca, for their feedback about various parts of the manuscript. I am very grateful to David Herman for his meticulous review of all the material and his astute insights.

My agent, Richard Pine, saw the value in my original proposal and helped guide and shape it for maximum effectiveness. Julie Rubenstein, my editor at Pocket Books, gave me the opportunity to fulfill my vision for this book. Her editorial instincts were invariably correct and significantly enhanced the final manuscript. Jane Cavolina's enthusiasm for this project which fell into her lap has been reassuring. The suggestions of my copy editor at Pocket Books, Sarah Haviland, were always on the mark. A final thank-you to all those I interviewed who offered their time and wisdom. My great-uncle, Simcha Cynamon, who gave his life so that his daughter and wife could escape death during the Holocaust remains a moral inspiration for me.

Printed in the United States
By Bookmasters